A JESUS WAY FORWARD

*Contemplative Discovery Through Story,
Scripture, and Spiritual Practice*

by

MARISA J. LAPISH

A Jesus Way Forward:
Contemplative Discovery Through Story, Scripture, and Spiritual Practice

Copyright © 2023 Marisa J. Lapish

Published by St. Macrina Press
Abbotsford, BC Canada

Scripture: Unless noted otherwise, scripture are quoted from the *Holy Bible, NIV* © International Bible Society. UBP of Zondervan.

Scripture quotations marked (NIV) are taken from the Holy Bible, New International Version®, NIV® Copyright © 1973, 1978, 1984 by International Bible Society. Used by permission of Zondervan. Publishing House. All rights reserved worldwide. www.zondervan.com

Emphases: All emphases throughout this book are the author's, including those in Scripture texts and cited material, unless otherwise indicated.

Printed in the United States

ISBN: 979-8-3918-9447-6

Author: Marisa J. Lapish, 1961–

Nonfiction > Religion > Christian Theology > Ethics

Book and Cover design: Laura Antonioli
Cover picture: Martino Pietropoli - Unsplash

St Macrina Press

TABLE OF CONTENTS

Marisa Lapish has written a real gem of a book on a beautifully articulated idea whose uniqueness demonstrates just how much it's needed in today's divided societies — namely, that it's possible to read the Scriptures in a way that nurtures our inner life and moves the compass needle toward genuine compassion and hospitality for the Other. By standing on the shoulders of the patristic giants before us, Lapish has gifted the lamentably all-too-often separated scholarly worlds of theology, hermeneutics, contemplation, and peacemaking with an enticing invitation to use the "rooted innovation" of ancient-future tools and approaches that heal wounds and help us discover the "ways of the Way" as nested in our own stories. This book is a much needed poetic and prophetic account of the Way to be read, absorbed, and circulated in churches, households, and communities that want to learn how to belong, be, and act in sacred dissent against our culture of oppressive power by instead honoring and amplifying marginal voices that we all need to hear and heed.

Andrew P. Klager, PhD
Professor of Religion and Peace Studies
Director of the Institute for Religion, Peace, and Justice
St. Stephen's University, (NB, Canada)

In this supremely helpful guide, Marisa Lapish calls us to engage and discover the "gospel of peace" exactly where it first emerged: in the prophetic voice of the marginalized. She helps us explore Scripture afresh by drawing together a Christ-focused hermeneutic, tried and true contemplative reflection, and a diverse community experience. In my view, Marisa's approach makes for richer and far healthier outcomes than what we've been seeing in our unraveling culture. Needful and wise!

Bradley Jersak
Dean of Theology & Culture
St. Stephen's University (NB, Canada)
Editor, CWR magazine / Clarion-Journal.com
Brad Jersak.com
Author, A More Christlike Word: Reading Scripture the Emmaus Way

Marisa Lapish writes, "the purpose of this book is to discover spiritually formational ways of reading scripture that lead to the embodiment of that contrasting Way in contemporary society." I think she pulled it off. This is a brilliant work, reflecting a comprehensive level of research and a beautiful wisdom that emerges from her own rich life experience. She turns the shame of a Christianity that seeks to dominate and colonize others into a tapestry of shared moments with people who live on the margins and have their own gifts to give.

Peter Fitch, D. Min.
Professor of Religious Studies and Historical Theology
St. Stephen's University, (St. Stephen, New Brunswick, Canada)

At the core of this work by Marisa Lapish is a desire to invite Christians together into a deeper, more authentic embodiment of the "Way": a certain posture of life, thoroughly grounded in the life and teachings of Christ, that shapes identity, community, and action in the world.

The "Way" (originally meaning Jesus as well as his followers) gave the early church its raison d'etre and established and curated its spiritual life and practices. From this context, Lapish provides a convincing portrait of the value and importance of practices such as radical inclusivity and hospitality (including feasts), various forms of contemplative prayer, and lectio divina. She also fleshes out and synthesizes what this could all look like practically by outlining and giving examples from the Discovery Bible Approach (DBS).

Ultimately, Lapish has a vision for the transformation of people, neighbourhoods, and contemporary society into thin places where Jesus and the new creation reside and flourish. In these places, everyone is welcomed and their story is honoured, people experience Jesus and increasingly desire to imitate him, those who are marginalized are included, and injustice is addressed and overturned.

Lapish has actually lived this kind of life herself, and it shows through her writing. She has devoted decades to working for peace, mercy, justice in her neighbourhood, has considered and embraced those who are marginalized, and integrated contemplative Christian spirituality and spiritual direction. She is an inspiration, calling us along with Jesus to embody the "Way" as we seek and pray for the kingdom and will of God to come and be done right here, right now. And to that, we say "Amen."

Suhail Stephen
Director, School of Mercy and Justice (Sustainable Faith)
Pastor, West End Abbey (Winnipeg, MB, Canada)
Teacher, School of Spiritual Direction (Sustainable Faith)
Spiritual Director

In a time of great critique of the church (and at times, rightfully so!), Lapish offers a refreshing view of what 'could be.' She does the thoughtful work for us of digging into the history and ancient roots of our spirituality to find what "the ways of the Way" of Jesus were and are. I found myself invited, awakened, and filled with imagination toward what felt like Jesus' loving intentions and desires for the church.

Sara Carlisle,
Director of Development
Sustainable Faith Europe/U.K.

Its object being infinite, the parameters of what constitutes theology or theological education have never been clearly discernible. Likewise, demarcating what is and is not "church" is a similarly nebulous project. Both from a distance and even from within, however, too many of us confuse the essence of theology and the work of the church with the elaborate structures that have evolved in their service over the past two millennia—the seminaries, the schools, the denominations, the liturgies, the traditions, etc. Valuable as these can be, Marisa Lapish wisely argues that contemporary folk interested in learning of God should look to the margins of these institutional spaces. Marisa's goal is not to demolish traditional practices or institutions, but to call readers to reorient themselves so that they can learn of God outside of spaces in which an infinite being cannot be contained. From the pen of a practitioner, here is a book that will help

God's people find a way to learn and worship without borders, and in doing so find themselves at the heart of the gospel story.

Michael Huffman
Author, Untie the Cords of Silence
Mozaik Center, Antalya, Turkey

The pandemic plus the events of 2020 accelerated what had been a slow and incremental journey of spiritual reformation for me. And it revealed that many other people were also on a similar journey of untangling Jesus and his teachings from western culture in order to see Jesus' teachings from other people's perspectives and reread scripture apart from cultural assumptions.

Marisa Lapish's book offers a path forward for the individual, the community, and theological educators for inviting followers of Jesus to come afresh to the pages of scripture, listen, observe, and dialogue with both the text and one another. She invites us into the ancient ways of engaging the text with renewed motivation for being formed by the God who inspired them.

Courtnee White
Cru City Neighbors Ministry (Northeast Ohio)

In her quest to discover and engage a contemplative spirituality that is more Christ-like and Spirit-led with potential for building local peace with her diverse neighbors, Marisa Lapish has immersed herself in multiple, small but diverse, organic gatherings of church with marginalized people. As a result she suggests a better way of being together as the church in all its expressions through a grassroots approach to spiritual formation that is communal, relationally connected, and Spirit-led. This is invaluable material for those concerned with the future of the church.

Rev. Dr. Hazel Partington
Congregational Care Pastor
Willoughby United Methodist Church (Willoughby, Ohio)
Author, Forgiveness Isn't Easy: But it is the Key to Freedom

For Jim, the love of my life

FOREWORD

In a recent virtual Q&A class with Brian McLaren that I moderated in a course I teach at St. Stephen's University called 'Religion, Peace and Conflict,' Brian told us about a Muslim friend of his who suggested that the verse in the Qu'ran that most Muslims point to for their understanding of how to relate to others who are different than them is Sura 49, verse 13, which reads that Allah has "made you into various nations and tribes so that you may know one another." In other words, difference is meant to stimulate our curiosity as a way to forge human bonds and perhaps even fill out in community what we lack as individuals. But as Brian pointed out through his own experience, the verse that Christians most often point to for the same reason is Jn. 14:6: "I am the way and the truth and the life. No one comes to the Father except through me." The former is an example of what I'd characterize as hospitable curiosity that honours the Other, and the latter is a verse that's been twisted into its opposite meaning by many Christians to give them a false sense superiority over others. Why this difference? Brian's friend answered this question with a very simple yet profound (and accurate) observation: We're taught this. Yet, as Marisa Lapish reminds us in this book, "the early Christian movement's spiritual momentum was empowered by the Holy Spirit and embodied through lovingkindness between diverse neighbors in local contexts."

The challenge, then, is this: when we have a polyvocal set of Scriptures to navigate, how do we identify and elevate the voice of the fully human One who asks us to care for the least of these and love our enemies and in whom *all* will be made alive? As challenging as this may seem and resistant to this we may sometimes be — whether because it takes too much effort or it takes too long — there's a strong sense that this can be fulfilled through, as St. Maximos the Confessor describes it, the crucifixion of the mind and by becoming fully human as God revealed full and true humanness on the Cross so that "I am crucified with Christ; and it is no longer I who live, but it is Christ who lives in me" (Gal. 2:20). What is needed then? In a word, *transformation*.

The book you hold in your hands advances a beautifully articulated idea whose uniqueness demonstrates just how much it's needed in today's divided societies — namely, that it's possible to read the Scriptures in a way that nurtures our inner life and moves the compass needle toward genuine compassion and hospitality for the Other. By standing on the shoulders of the patristic giants before us, Marisa has gifted the lamentably all-too-often separated scholarly worlds of theology, hermeneutics, contemplation, and peacemaking with an enticing invitation to use the "rooted innovation" of ancient-future tools and approaches that heal wounds and help us discover the "ways of the Way" as nested in our own stories. This book is a much-needed poetic and prophetic account of the Way to be read, absorbed, and circulated in churches, households, and communities that want to learn how to belong, be, and act in sacred dissent against our culture of oppressive power by instead honoring and amplifying marginal voices that we all need to hear and heed.

We are transformed then by the kenotic power from below that's exhibited by the outcasts, oppressed, and marginalized who are becoming human through the same cross-bearing that also revealed God Incarnate as truly and fully human. And this transformation through the cultivation of the divine virtues of humility, patience, poverty of spirit, meekness, and peace becomes the hermeneutical key for unlocking the voice of the One who's ushering in "a more just and peaceable kingdom of God culture in grassroots local contexts through organic expressions of the Jesus Way." Marisa invites us to join her on this pilgrimage through the soul-penetrating words that she offers us in this book, all the while reminding us that, in the prophetic words of Karl Rahner, "The Christian of the future will be a mystic or he will not exist at all" — yet whose mysticism also motivates, shapes, and animates, as Marisa suggests, "a radically inclusive hospitality, full of love for God and embracing love for neighbor" and an "enfleshed Jesus Way lifestyle." I am so glad this book was written and just as glad that you are now about to read it!

Memento mori +

Andrew Phillip Klager

INTRODUCTION

At its onset, the Christian movement was a marginal one, identified as followers of the Way—Jesus Christ.[1] Followers of Jesus were distinguished by how their collective lifestyle resembled "the *Jesus Way* as lived and taught by Jesus Christ."[2] Their approach to this new way of life was characterized by absolute devotion to enfleshing the kingdom of God that Jesus described in the Sermon on the Mount: on earth as it is in heaven.[3] In Acts, the early Christian movement's spiritual momentum was empowered by the Holy Spirit and embodied through lovingkindness between diverse neighbors in local contexts. A specific pattern emerged during this early movement, as Jesus Way followers repeatedly gathered, spiritually connected, and then scattered throughout the wider region before beginning the cycle again. The Jesus Way was communal and prayerful, oriented toward apostolic teaching and centered on the "breaking of bread."[4] At the same time, the Jesus Way moved—spontaneously and organically, with rapid expansion brought to life through spirit-empowered gifts via a radically inclusive hospitality, full of love for God and embracing love for neighbor. Persecution from outside the movement and division from within powerfully scattered the loosely connected gatherings of followers by the Holy Spirit across the known world as we see penned across the New Testament writings. Nonetheless, what was it about the orientation of the Jesus Way community—their approach toward God, each other, and their neighbors—that incarnated into their spiritual practice and

---

1 John Chrysostom, *Catena on the Acts of the Apostles* 19.9 (CGPNT 3:315), quoted in Francis Martin (ed.) and Thomas C. Oden (gen. ed.), *Acts: Ancient Christian Commentary on Scripture, NT V* (Downers Grove, IL: InterVarsity Press, 2006), p. 236. Chrysostom notes: "Fittingly do they call this 'the way' as it truly was the way that leads to the kingdom of heaven. Or the Scripture is saying that Christ is the way, as he is called the way, or it is speaking of the true faith, that which is proclaimed through Paul, by which any wayfarer arrives at the kingdom of heaven."

2 Bradley Jersak, *A More Christlike Way: A More Beautiful Faith* (Pasadena, CA: Plain Truth Ministries, 2019), p. 21.

3 Ibid.; Matthew 5-7 (NIV).

4 Acts 2: 42-47.

practical outworking of the Jesus Way in their communities? What were the "ways" of the Jesus Way?

As a graduate student immersed in ancient Christian history, I noticed that while scholars wrestled with questions of orthodoxy as Christianity was institutionalized over centuries, outlying groups of Christ followers resisted the status quo institutional churches and formed communities for spiritual engagement with God while loving the poor and the marginalized people in their cultures.[5] At times, such groups were also marginalized and persecuted, and their influence was minimized by the institutional Church of the time. As prophetic voices of dissent,[6] these communities called back to remembrance the Jesus Way to be lived in their present world with a finger pointing forward as a Kingdom of God reminder of what has yet to fully come. How might today's expressions of the Jesus Way in the margins also prophetically move the "Church-in-the-center" forward in its kingdom of God trajectory?

Similarly, the current cultural milieu of global pandemic and racial strife seems to be having a scattering effect on the religious institutions of Church and Academy. In the contemplative, liminal space of pandemic, where the world has been forced to de-center gatherings of institutional church and theological education into online or at-home formats, many people have exited traditional spiritual spaces. In light of this movement, a diverse group of theological scholars and educators gathered their ideas together "for critical, theological conversations about the meanings and

---

5   Examples of prophetically dissenting marginal communities in Christian history include the desert fathers and mothers of the 4th-5th centuries, Brothers and Sisters of the Common Life and the beguinages in the 14th-15th centuries; Count Zinzendorf and Herrnhut in the 18th century; Dietrich Bonhoeffer and the Finkenwalde community in the 20th century; and the New Monasticism movement of the 21st century. For examination of these movements, see Gerald L. Sittser, *Water from a Deep Well: Christian Spirituality From Early Martyrs to Modern Missionaries* (Downers Grove, IL: IVP Books, 2007), pp. 80-81; Justo L. Gonzalez, *The Story of Christianity: The Early Church to the Present Day Vol 1* (Peabody, MA: Prince Press, 2001), pp. 357-359; Gonzalez, *The Story of Christianity Vol 2*, pp. 208-209; Dietrich Bonhoeffer, *Life Together* (New York: Harper & Row Publishers, 1954), pp. 10-11; Alden Bass, "Bringing It To Completion: American New Monastics and the Benedictine Tradition," *American Benedictine Review* 66 (2015): 352-363.
6   Walter Brueggemann, *The Prophetic Imagination* (Minneapolis: Fortress Press, 2012), p. 55.

purposes of theological education in a time of deep change."[7] They jointly published "between the times," books released in 2020-2022 as reflective critiques to thoughtfully reorient ideas about theological education for the church of the future. Their insights are profound, timely, and quite unanimous concerning spiritual formation. At the same time, the quiet and hidden organic margins of the Jesus Way "live and move and have their being"[8] around the globe in rapidly growing "Disciple-Making Movements"[9] across cultures in the Global South and East. What might the institutional expressions of the Jesus Way learn from these diverse grassroots groups of Jesus followers about a more Christlike, embodied spirituality?

The research presented here encompasses a broad spectrum of sources that otherwise might not share common space for a mutually enriching dialogue for the future of the Jesus Way. Contemporary marginal voices that prophetically enflesh and envision spiritual formation in fresh, new ways are amplified in the same pages as university professors, grassroots practitioners, and ancient voices, enabling readers to listen transcendently beyond the theological boundaries that we create. Rather than suffocating in our self-made, sound-proof echo chambers, we can choose to step outside of them to take a deep breath in the spacious written pages where others have found the Jesus Way and learn freely and fearlessly from each other. In so doing, might we be transformed by reading scripture more contemplatively with open listening postures and mutual storytelling with our neighbors? Might we begin to embody the radical and self-giving spirituality that Jesus taught and modeled in the Sermon on the Mount together as we open our homes and hospitable spaces for these new, local gatherings? Might we learn to love God more deeply by authentically living a more peaceful love ethic with our diverse neighbors?

---

7   Ted A. Smith (ed.), *Theological Education Between the Times Book Series* (Grand Rapids, MI: William B. Eerdmans Publishing Company, 2020-2022). Quote from inside the series' book covers.

8   Acts 17:28.

9   David L. Watson and Paul D. Watson, *Contagious Disciplemaking: Leading Others on a Journey of Discovery* (Nashville, TN: Thomas Nelson, 2014), pp. xi-xvi.

This book first briefly examines the theological origin story of the early followers of Jesus in the book of Acts, exploring its approach to gathering and expanding its cultural influence to determine what defined its identity as a marginal group. During significant eras of Christian history, the existence of outlying marginal groups of Jesus followers acting as prophetic voices of dissent to the institutional Church revitalized its movement in history. We see another such moment now. By acknowledging that our present cultural milieu of global pandemic signifies an "in between" space for theological reflection and praxis for change, this book offers summaries of contemporary scholarly research in a wide range of theological institutions for insights into present day issues affecting spiritual formation and the future of the Church. Next, this book amplifies the prophetic witness of the diverse organic Disciple-Making Movement in the Global South and East, which began over twenty years ago. By exploring inclusive, radical hospitality in the margins, ancient spiritual formation practices for interpreting scripture, and time-honored contemplative prayer practices, the book presents an ancient-future reorientation for facilitating a more Christlike, embodied spirituality. This enfleshed Jesus Way lifestyle must be practiced among diverse neighbors to foster a more just and peaceable kingdom of God culture in grassroots local contexts through organic expressions of the Jesus Way. This book integrates research and application to present an accessible model for Jesus Way followers to encourage communal spiritual transformation as a non-coercive means to love both God and neighbors. This restorative spirituality is embodied as neighbors show hospitality, practice mutuality in dialogic scripture reading and contemplative prayer, and break bread together in homes—all defining characteristics of the Jesus Way over history.

On a personal note, I have followed Jesus as the Way for forty years. Over those years (and still today), I have been involved in a variety of embodied grassroots expressions of church and theological education, including neighborhood Bible studies, house churches, Discovery Bible Studies in immigrant communities, and alternative justice-oriented theological education cohorts. Concurrently, I also embrace the beauty of the institutional church to worship and serve in more traditional theological education spaces and local churches in my region. I believe that we are living in an unprecedented time in the history of the global Church to consider our theological responsibility to embody the alternative peaceable kingdom of God to bless the world with neighborly love through the beloved community of Jesus followers, in *all* of its beautiful expressions—organic and institutional. My hope and prayer is that readers will be inspired with the life-giving breath of the Spirit—revived—to embody the "ways of the Jesus Way," offering the winsome, self-giving love of Jesus to wayfarers.

CHAPTER I

THE JESUS WAY

Gathered and Scattered Beloved Community

Fourth century church father, John Chrysostom, presents his quandary about the term referring to Jesus followers as "the Way" in one of the earliest written commentaries for this description in Acts 19:9. "Fittingly do they call this 'the way,' as it truly was the way that leads to the kingdom of heaven. Or the Scripture is saying that Christ is the way, as he is called the way, or it is speaking of the true faith, that which is proclaimed through Paul, by which any wayfarer arrives at the kingdom of heaven."[10] Jesus undeniably referred to himself as "the Way" in John 14:6, and it is worth beginning the study of his namesake community by exploring how Jesus taught and embodied the meaning of this term. The Greek word, *hodos,* is used in scripture to identify both Jesus *and* Jesus-followers as "the Way" to emphasize a "manner of life or action" which defines each referent and identifies the referents with each other through a common *approach* to life, a *way of belonging, being, and acting* in the world.[11]

Historically, Jesus walked out his earthly life in first century Palestine within the context of Jewish culture in the Roman Empire. N.T. Wright asserts that Jesus' calling was "to renew and restore the people of Israel."[12] He did so living a life of marginality. He lived as a poor, homeless Jew; he

---

10 John Chrysostom, *Catena,* p. 236.

11 Spiros Zodhiates and Warren Baker, (eds.), *Hebrew-Greek Key Word Study Bible: NIV* (Chattanooga, TN: AMG Publishers, 1996): p. 1654. The Greek *hodos* (3487) is used for Jesus as "the Way" (John 14:6) and Jesus' followers as "the Way" (Acts 9:2; 19:9, 23; 24:14, 22); See also Diana Butler Bass, *Christianity After Religion: The End of the Church and the Birth of a New Spiritual Awakening,* (New York: HarperOne, 2012), pp. 204-214. Similarly, Bass refers to a sequentially ordered pattern of belonging, behaving, and believing in her book.

12 N.T. Wright, *Acts for Everyone: Part 1* (Louisville, KY: Westminster John Knox Press, 2008), p. 6.

was "a member of a minority group in the midst of a larger dominant and controlling group."[13] Jesus chose a motley group of twelve disenfranchised disciples, representing the twelve tribes of Israel,[14] to follow him in his purpose to transform "things within this world, bringing the sphere of earth into the presence, and under the rule, of heaven itself."[15]

Jesus' initial call to his disciples was to follow him; belief was not a prerequisite. They literally followed him—physically traversing the soils and seas of first century Palestine. The disciples gathered around Jesus and those with whom he associated most closely, which included the poor, weak, outcast, foreigners, and prostitutes.[16] Jesus taught orally and performatively; he was not a writer.[17] He taught privately and publicly through story, parable, paradox, miracle, ritual, discussion, questioning, and silence.[18] The scenes of his instruction included homes with tables, boats on lakes, gardens and roads, fields and deserts.[19]

The faith of the disciples began with following him, belonging to each other in community and "enacting the practices of God's way." Proclamation of the kingdom of God followed belonging and behavior.[20] Their belief grew out of their togetherness, "praying, eating, preaching, healing, giving, and feeding" as they gathered to practice a radical hospitality with diverse people on the margins of the religious and political mainstream.[21]

Jesus set out to gather a scattered Israel that was fragmented into divisive groups, so "he went to tax collectors and Zealots, to the poor and to the rich, to the rural population of Galilee and to the capital city of Jerusa-

---

13   Howard Thurman, *Jesus and the Disinherited* (Boston: Beacon Press, 1976), p. 8.

14   Wright, *Acts*, p. 6.

15   Ibid., p. 8.

16   Yvette Flunder, *Where the Edge Gathers: Building a Community of Radical Inclusion* (Cleveland, OH: The Pilgrim Press, 2005), p. 2.

17   Mark Jordan, *Transforming Fire: Imagining Christian Teaching* (Grand Rapids, MI: William B. Eerdmans Publishing Company, 2021), pp. 15-17, 22.

18   Ibid., p. 26,

19   Ibid., p. 16.

20   Diana Butler Bass, *Christianity After Religion: The End of Church and the Birth of a New Spiritual Awakening*, (New York: HarperOne, 2012), p. 209.

21   Ibid., p. 208.

lem."[22] He sent out his disciples to do the same, scattering the seed of the "already and not yet" kingdom of God to herald good news for all people. The inbreaking kingdom of God was demonstrated by mighty works, like healing the sick, feeding the hungry, and breaking the chains of demonic prisons. These were the signs that the reign of God was already present and that in the future eschaton: "no one may be excluded from salvation: not outsiders, not sinners, not the sick."[23] Jesus' community life was not invisible, states Lohfink.[24] The Jesus Way was not an ethereal religion of spiritual purity. The beloved community of Jesus followers was an embodied one of eating and drinking with sinners, of physically healing and socially restoring sick people.[25] Nor was "his bloody death on the cross…

---

22   Gerhard Lohfink, *Jesus and Community: The Social Dimension of Christian Faith*, trans. John P. Galvin (Philadelphia: Fortress Press, 1984), p. 12.

23   Ibid., pp. 14; 87-89. Lohfink explains that Jesus' preaching of the kingdom of God was closely connected to miracles of healing, and it was a socially reconciliatory phenomenon. "It was characteristic that he constantly established community—precisely for those who were denied community at that time, or who were judged inferior in respect to religion. Jesus made clear through his word and even more through his concrete conduct that he did not recognize religious-social exclusion and discrimination." (p.88). By preaching the kingdom of God, Jesus sought to heal the dualities of rich/poor (Luke 19:1-10; Luke 6:20), educated/uneducated (Luke 14:1-6; Matthew 11:25-26), rural/urban (Mark 1:14; Matthew 23:37), healthy/sick (Matthew 4:23), just/sinners (Mark 2:17; Luke 19:10) because in God's kingdom no one is disqualified, and all are recipients. Jesus especially stood in solidarity with groups that were "denied equality or even refused community in contemporary Jewish society" such as the poor (Luke 7:22), the hungry (Luke 6:21), those mourning (Luke 6:21), burdened (Matthew 11:28), the ill (Mark 3:1-6), sinners (Mark 2:17), tax collectors (Matthew 11:19), prostitutes (Matthew 21:31-32), Samaritans (Luke 10:25-37), women (Matthew 5:31-32), and children (Mark 10:13-16). (p. 88-89).

24   Ibid., p. 28.

25   Phuc Luu, *Jesus of the East: Reclaiming the Gospel for the Wounded* (Harrisonburg, VA: Herald Press, 2020), pp. 84-85; 99-101. Luu explains that Jesus came to bring wholeness and healing to 'sinners.' "Within Jesus' own culture, the term *sinner* was applied by the oppressors to those whom they saw as 'other.' Their list of 'sinners' was mainly made up of people who were laborers. Prostitutes were included because of their promiscuity, but so were shepherds, whose work kept them from observing the Sabbath, and butchers and leather tanners, whose work required them to deal in blood, making them ritually unclean." (p. 85) The term 'sinner' was used as a religious slur for the "other." Religious leaders considered these people improper or impure according to the Jewish purity laws, but Jesus identified with them and socially included those considered 'sinners' by eating and drinking with them and by healing them. He did so to demonstrate "that sin is neither inherent to their being nor incurable. They simply need healing…" (p. 99-100) In other words, the sick were the ones being sinned against since they were oppressed by religious laws that religious leaders created and interpreted as exclusionary according to the good/bad, holy/unclean dichotomies of purity systems. Jesus came "to bring healing to them, to liberate them from the oppression of those who would impose that burden on them." (p. 101)

an invisible event."[26] Jesus' banded disciples and their ministry together was a visible encapsulation of the future reign of God embodied through a small group of diverse, marginalized people in their present cultural milieu. Eberhard Arnold stated that Jesus "…prophesied a kingdom, a rule of God which was to change completely the conditions and order of the world and make them new."[27]

Jesus warned that the living kingdom of God disrupts the cultural social order, and this is displayed most radically within the way followers would gather together communally as a *new family* within the Roman context of the ancient patriarchal family. Lohfink highlights that God was now their *abba* father, and that "patriarchal domination is no longer permissible in the family, but only motherliness, fraternity, and childlikeness before God the Father."[28] In the beloved community, structures and relationships of domination were not permitted, nor honorific titles.[29] Instead, service out of self-giving love would be central in the new family ethics.[30] As a family of peace, the new family of Jesus' brothers and sisters would gather hospitably as servants of all—a visible, experiential, and tangible alternative society already ruled by Love pointing forward to the future kingdom where all would be rightly restored. A theocracy was not the intention. The alternative social order instead would become a means of subversive prophetic dissent to upend the violent structures and powers of the Roman Empire. The new family would be a *contrast-society*, in the words of Lohfink, implying self-giving service instead of domination, peaceful restorative justice instead of violent retribution, described by Jesus in his Sermon on the Mount.[31]

---

26   Ibid.
27   Eberhard Arnold, *Salt and Light: Living the Sermon on the Mount,* (Walden, NY: Plough Publishing House, 1998), p. xviii. Eberhard Arnold founded a community based on the Sermon on the Mount called Bruderhof in 1920.
28   Lohfink, *Jesus and Community,* pp. 48-49.; Note: According to Lohfink, "The disciples will find everything again in the new family of God, brothers and sisters, mothers and children; but they will find fathers no longer." (p. 49); see also Mark 10:30.
29   Ibid., p. 46; see also Matthew 23:8-12.
30   Luke 22:26.
31   Lohfink, *Jesus and Community,* pp. 50-56, 70-73.

Jesus' kingdom of God manifesto is encompassed in his Sermon on the Mount teaching in Matthew 5-7. Moore highlights that "Jesus begins the Sermon on the Mount announcing that those who have suffered are seen."[32] Eberhard Arnold interprets the beatitudes with similar empathetic solidarity:

> Blessed are those who have heart. Blessed are those who love, who build up unity everywhere. Blessed are those who stand with the poor; blessed are those who themselves are poor as beggars. Blessed are those who know themselves as beggars before the Spirit. Blessed are those who are so poor that they hunger and thirst. Blessed are those who feel this hunger and thirst for justice, for the justice of the heart, of love, for the establishment of peace in unity. For they are the people who carry the pain of the world on their hearts, who carry the suffering of the world in their inmost being. They do not think of themselves, for their whole heart is turned toward others. Yet they are the people who are misunderstood and persecuted because they love justice and do not take part in injustice. That is why they are the salt of the earth.[33]

Jesus embodied the Beatitudes[34], demonstrating how the reign of God on earth is made visible as an embodied icon—a window painted with flesh and blood through which to gaze with hope into the future restoration of all things. The Sermon on the Mount subverts social order to dismantle power differentials and domination, through a nonviolent and peaceable love ethic which defines the ways of the kingdom.[35] The

---

32 Osheta Moore, *Dear White Peacemakers: Dismantling Racism With Grit and Grace* (Harrisonburg, VA: Herald Press, 2021), p. 39.

33 Arnold, *Salt and Light*, pp. 4-5.

34 Chris E. W. Green, *Sanctifying Interpretation: Vocation, Holiness, and Scripture;* 2nd ed. (Cleveland, TN: CPT Press, 2020), p. 38.

35 Moore, *Dear White Peacemakers*, pp. 37-39.

kingdom of God begins already as "enemies are loved, the last penny is given away, and violence is never repaid with force. Purity and faithfulness belong to love. This is the better righteousness, complete love."[36]

The central message in the teachings of Jesus is love.[37] A childlike spirit of love reigns and rules relationally.[38] Jesus interprets Jewish Law with a just and merciful hermeneutic in his sermon, turning religious tables of interpretation with his "You have heard it said…but I say to you" statements, while ethically demonstrating in physical actions how the Law and Prophets are fulfilled in him. The Great Commandment of loving God and loving neighbor in Matthew 22:36-40 fulfills *all* the Law and the Prophets, says Jesus, while he embodied that very *way* of love expressed through compassionate action. Green pointedly states, "Loving God is inseparable from loving neighbor. In fact, loving our neighbor just *is* the way we love God."[39]

Jesus definitively demonstrated this "self-giving, radically forgiving, co-suffering love" for God, neighbor, and enemy alike through his cruciform death on the cross.[40] Jersak emphasizes, "Jesus Christ showed us, in person, that God is Love. Period."[41] Jesus substantiated his love by offering his own body, soul, and spirit for the bodies, souls, and spirits of humanity.[42] His resurrection demonstrated bodily transformation as the onset of God's new creation. "Jesus' risen body is…the beginning of a heavenly reality which is fully at home on, and in, this physical world ('earth'), and the beginning of a transformed world which is fully at home in God's sphere."[43] Wright insists there is no gospel without the resurrection.[44]

---

36   Arnold, *Salt and Light*, p. 146.
37   Obery Hendricks, *Christians Against Christianity: How Right-Wing Evangelicals Are Destroying Our Nation and Our Faith* (Boston: Beacon Press, 2021), p. 1.; see also Howard Thurman, *Jesus and the Disinherited*, p. 79.
38   Arnold, *Salt and Light*, p. 3.
39   Green, *Sanctifying Interpretation*, p. 40.
40   Jersak, *A More Christlike Way*, p. 27.
41   Ibid.
42   Arnold, *Salt and Light*, p. 150.
43   Wright, *Acts*, p. 4.
44   Ibid.

In the forty days following the resurrection, Jesus continued teaching his followers about the kingdom of God. While he was eating with them, he instructed them to gather and wait together for the Holy Spirit's coming, foretelling a scattering to the ends of the earth. Abruptly, Jesus ascended into the heavens, leaving his followers as the continued expression of "the Jesus Way" led by the power of the Spirit of Jesus to move in the world which remained firmly under their feet.[45] In the context of scripture and prayer, the new family gathered to wait communally, and on Pentecost day, the disruptive Holy Spirit came with power. Jennings interprets the incoming Spirit as a collapse of human aspirations for an earthly kingdom of domination into Jesus himself as the Way of life—"a new cultural politic of *joining*."[46]

Jennings describes this "new way" [as] "a *joining* that brings stories, hopes, and life in a shared work of knowing, remembering, and testifying."[47] This certainly is evident in Acts 2 where, in a grand reversal of Babel, languages formerly separated and scattered were joined together for understanding the "wonders of God" by the Holy Spirit, causing both amazement and questions to rise in human hearts.[48] Through the initiating movement of the Holy Spirit, this joining progressively manifests throughout the book of Acts organically through gathering and scattering, through sowing and reaping. The good news subversively spreads with mustard seed-like growth throughout first century, Roman-ruled Palestine by a small group of marginalized people named "the Way," who actively follow the Spirit of Jesus after his ascension.[49] Jennings further elaborates,

> The Spirit is crumbling imperial design from within by destroying the divide between those enslaved and their masters. The hierarchies nurtured so carefully by the Ro-

---

45 Acts 1: 1-14.
46 Willie James Jennings, *Acts: A Theological Commentary on the Bible* (Louisville, KY: Westminster John Knox Press, 2017), p. 22.
47 Ibid., p. 24.
48 Acts 2: 1-12.
49 Acts 9:2; Acts 19: 9, 23; Acts 24: 14, 22.

man Empire are being undone by the Spirit, who will not release slave or free, Jew or Gentile, to their own self-interpretations but who will relentlessly prod them to open themselves toward one another in a life that builds the common. Now in the Spirit the common is not the bottom, not the despised humble beginning, and not the launching pad into social and economic hierarchies. It is the goal of life together with God. The common is the condition of a joined life where the haves and the have-nots are bound together in clear sight of one another and in shared support. The common is the redistribution of life where the Spirit invites us to a sharing of space and place, resources and dreams. The common takes from empire its designs for building a world and from diaspora its plans for surviving it. Instead, the common joins, weaving together purpose and hope in the life of discipleship to Jesus.[50]

In the beginning chapters of Acts, we get a glimpse of the spiritual practices that the Holy Spirit was inspiring in the gatherings of followers which further identified them as "the Way." The Way was a "community of practice."[51] The spiritual practices, defined and enfleshed by Jesus as the Way, manifest in communal, ethical living to demonstrate the anticipated reign of love and justice. "Practices are the connective tissue between what is, what can be, and what will be. Spiritual practices are living pictures of God's intentions for a world of love and justice."[52]

In his commentary on Acts 2:42-47, Wright maps out the four insep-arable spiritual practices of the Jesus Way as: "the apostles' teaching; the common life of those who believed; the breaking of the bread; and the prayers."[53] He stresses the interconnectivity of these practices. None of

---

50   Jennings, *Acts*, pp. 9-10.
51   Bass, *Christianity After Religion*, p. 207.
52   Ibid., p. 160.
53   Wright, *Acts*, p. 44.

these four practices could be ignored without detriment to the manifestation of the kingdom of love that the gatherings of the Jesus Way represented.[54] The apostles' teaching displayed the Way of Scripture in light of the fulfillment of the Law and the Prophets through the life, death, and resurrection of its *telos*,[55] Jesus, whom they followed as the Way. Their common life made visible the *new family*, who upset social, political, and religious systems of power to make peaceably clear that the new kingdom's ways were to love, share, and serve. This lay in stark contrast with the pervasive violence, violation, and domination prevalent in the surrounding culture of the Empire. Central to these gatherings is the pinnacle expression of Jesus' death and resurrection, the 'breaking of the bread', which reveals the self-giving, co-suffering, radically forgiving, and unifying love of God through common bread and wine around a table of beloved brothers and sisters.[56] The spiritual practice of prayer, as Jesus modeled it as "thy kingdom come, thy will be done, on earth as it is in heaven,"[57] only makes sense with the kingdom idea that "heaven and earth are designed to be joined together, and we can share in that already."[58]

Significantly, these relatively small and simply formed liturgical gatherings of the family of God moved into homes where social, ethnic, religious, and gender barriers were broken. Lohfink cites Stuhlmacher's observations that these important imperial barriers in the ancient world were broken in homes through binding people to Christ and each other with diversity "as the 'new creation', that is, the anticipatory sign of the new world of God, and of the necessity and reality of a new life."[59] Lohfink identifies the New Testament communities by the following characteris-

---

54 Ibid., p. 44-47.
55 Peter Enns, "Apostolic Hermeneutics and an Evangelical Doctrine of Scripture: Moving Beyond a Modernistic Impasse," *WTJ* 65 (2003): 277. Peter Enns developed the term, "christotelic" to refer to a Christ-driven hermeneutic which, for the church, sees the Old Testament as a whole finding its consummation (*telos*) in Christ, with a trajectory continuing in the church today.
56 Marisa Lapish, "The Lord's Supper Table as Icon of Remembrance," *Kenarchy Journal* 3.7 (2022): 133-143. Available online: https://kenarchy.org/wp-content/uploads/2022/01/kenarchy_Volume3.7.pdf; accessed: February 16, 2022.
57 Matthew 5:9-13.
58 Wright, *Acts*, p. 45.
59 Lohfink, *Jesus and Community*, citing Stuhlmacher, p. 98.

tics: their conduct as the people of God; the presence of the Holy Spirit; the elimination of social barriers; the praxis of 'togetherness' (expressed in language of 'one another' admonitions); a new family love; the renunciation of domination; their purpose as a contrast-society and as a sign for the nations.[60]

Evidence that this fourfold pattern of spiritual practice continued into the second century is recorded by Justin Martyr in his travel journal from Asia Minor to Rome in 150 CE "All those who live in the city or the country gather together in one place on the day of the sun, and the memoirs of the apostles or the writings of the prophets are read…Then we all rise together and pray; and then…bread and wine and water are brought."[61] The written witness of early church fathers in later centuries testified to the continued prominence of these spiritual practices where followers were "united with each other in communion with the one Holy Spirit,"[62] as "a foundation of love, and a comfort to poverty, and a corrective of riches, and an occasion of the highest philosophy, and an instruction of humility"[63] in their gatherings.[64]

Scriptural instruction was conveyed throughout the New Testament—by Jesus and his followers—by retelling and reframing the stories of the Hebrew Bible with Jesus as its fulfillment, or *telos*. Brueggemann states that the good news is reenacted in the narrative of the texts and that the "stories themselves are vehicles whereby all things are made new."[65] He continues, "I mean to suggest that there is no single narrative in the Bible that is the normative account of the "news" (even as the early church leaves us with four Gospel accounts, and not one single normative one).

---

60   Ibid., pp. 75-147.
61   Justin Martyr, *First Apology* 67, trans. Marcus Dods and George Reith (Moscow, ID: Roman Roads Media, 2015), p. 45.
62   Maximus the Confessor, quoted in Gennadios Limouris "The Eucharist as the Sacrament of Sharing: An Orthodox Point of View," *The Ecumenical Review* (1986), p. 403.
63   John Chrysostom, *Homily 27 on First Corinthians,* (2) I Corinthians 11:17.
64   Lapish, "The Lord's Supper Table," pp. 133-143. See article for additional patristic views on the practice of the Eucharist including those footnoted above (Justin Martyr, Maximus the Confessor, John Chrysostom).
65   Walter Brueggemann, *Biblical Perspectives on Evangelism: Living in a Three-Storied Universe* (Nashville: Abingdon Press, 1993), p. 11.

Rather there are characteristic re-tellings that take a variety of forms, told with constancy, but with considerable imagination and complexity."[66] Diana Butler Bass similarly contends that "Jesus' followers did not sit around a fire and listen to lectures on Christian theology. They listened to stories that taught them how to act toward one another, what to do in the world."[67] Justin Martyr called the apostolic stories, "memoirs."[68]

Likewise, the New Testament documents the writers' interpretive struggles through their own wrestling with sacred text and religious traditions, empire and diaspora, culture and ethics. They wrestled, reenacted, and reframed in real time and space together and some of them wrote spiritual memoirs about their communal journey[69] as they followed the Spirit of Jesus to new places of geography and spiritual dilemma. The faithfulness of the community was defined by their practice of loving God and neighbor. "Early Christians judged ethical failings as the most serious breach of community, even as they accepted a significant amount of theological diversity in their midst."[70] The epistles are not void of descriptions of divisions within the church itself that, no doubt, had a scattering effect on the followers of Jesus.

The spiritually embodied example of the Jesus Way—how they interpreted scriptures and lived out its love-ethic, how they prayed, how they embodied their common life together, and how they scattered around the world proclaiming the gospel while revealing Jesus in the breaking of the bread—is noteworthy. The embodied, communal spiritual practices centered on Jesus as the Way and were lived in community and among neighbors, causing a resounding stir whereby Tertullian famously exclaimed, "Look how they love one another!"[71] As the gospel was scattered

---

66   Ibid., p. 12.
67   Bass, *Christianity After Religion*, p. 207.
68   Justin Martyr, *First Apology* 67, p. 45.
69   Bass, *Christianity After Religion*, p. 179.
70   Ibid., p. 149.
71   Tertullian, *Apology* 39, quoted in Rodney Stark, *The Rise of Christianity: How the Obscure, Marginal Jesus Movement Became the Dominant Religious Force in the Western World in a Few Centuries* (San Francisco: HarperSanFrancisco, 1997), p. 87.

like seed into new geographical locations in the diaspora, new gatherings were formed as followers of Jesus multiplied.

Through the rest of Acts, Spirit-empowered followers were referred to as the Way, defined not only by the "ways" of their gathered identity but by their outward, scattering movement. The small beginnings of the Jesus Way in Jerusalem in 30 CE (Acts 1:1-7:60) scattered to Judea and Samaria from 30-43 CE (Acts 8:1-11:18), to spread throughout the Roman Empire in 43-62 CE (Acts 11:19-28:31) by the end of the book of Acts.[72] This scattering was caused largely by the gospel proclamation through its embodied messengers as the Jesus Way. The contrast-society disrupted the social, religious, political, and cultural status quo by the power of the Holy Spirit. As the "already but not yet" reign of God invaded the world through the Jesus Way, religious, political, social, economic, and emotional persecution ensued in practically every chapter of Acts.[73]

Sober reflection on the effects of prophetic dissent that embodying the Jesus Way had on the surrounding culture will note that the resulting persecution and its marginalizing and scattering effects provided opportunities for witness, or *martys*.[74] Penner relates,

> The testimony of Acts is not so much that persecution causes church growth but that church growth and the spread of the gospel tend to cause persecution, as religious and political leaders rise up and try to stop this movement that has "caused trouble all over the world and has now come here" (Acts 17:6)[75]

As the Jesus Way gradually became more institutionalized over time, the Church itself became the perpetrator of persecution at times, further

---

72   Glenn M. Penner, *In the Shadow of the Cross: A Biblical Theology of Persecution and Discipleship* (Bartlesville, OK: Living Sacrifice Books, 2004), p. 156.

73   Ibid., pp. 162-163; See Acts 4; 5; 7; 8; 9; 12; 13; 14:1-7, 14:8-22; 16; 17:1-12; 17:13-34; 18; 19; 21-23.

74   Sittser, *Water from a Deep Well*, p. 33.

75   Penner, *In the Shadow*, p. 162.

scattering the seed to sprout newly formed organic gatherings in the margins.

CHAPTER 2

ANOTHER WAY

Prophetic Dissent Embodied in the Margins

The gathering and scattering movement continued to grow as evidenced throughout the rest of the New Testament story. The epistles attest that the movement was catapulted by the persecution, with apostolic writers strengthening and encouraging Jesus Way followers to remain faithful within the contrasting culture of violence and domination in the Roman Empire.[76] Gonzalez confirms "two-and-a-half centuries of persecution by the Roman Empire, from the time of Nero to the conversion of Constantine."[77] At times, Christians were scapegoated as a marginal group as when being charged with arson for a great fire in Rome in 64 CE.[78] Their inclusivity made them suspect by the Roman government. The waves of persecution were stirred by rumors about the specific ways in which they gathered communally as an expansive and egalitarian group that shared resources.[79] The new family of brothers and sisters "drew a picture of Christian worship as an orgiastic, celebration in which Christians ate and drank to excess, put the lights out, and vented their lusts in indiscriminate and even incestuous unions."[80] Their communion practice, with its expression of eating the body and blood, likewise gave rise to accusations of cannibalism.[81]

---

76   Ibid., pp. 169-260.
77   Gonzalez, *The Story of Christianity*, p. 33.
78   Ibid., pp. 33-34.
79   Phuc Luu, *Jesus of the East*, pp. 33-34.
80   Gonzalez, *The Story of Christianity*, p. 50.
81   Ibid.

The dynamic interaction of history with culture also contributed to the scattering of followers of the Jesus Way. Historically, the movement was propelled by the emotional and religious connectivity of the Jewish diaspora, the common language of *koine* Greek, and the accessibility of the Roman road system as trade routes. These cultural realities and technological advances favored the proclamatory spread of the gospel to new regions, by missionaries like Paul and Barnabas, as well as by countless and nameless followers that included the enslaved, merchants, and other travelers.[82] At the same time, Stark asserts the existence of "extraordinary levels of urban disorder, social dislocation, filth, disease, misery, fear, and cultural chaos" as distinctive characteristics of the cities in which Christianity arose, and suggests that the early movement became a solution to these societal problems.[83]

In the context of hospitality, the Jesus Way offered safety and refuge not only for the persecuted, but also for any needy person.[84] The mutuality of practical love expressed through the shared resources in the ethnically diverse gatherings of both the privileged and poor women and men of the Jesus Way collapsed social dichotomies, mitigating social relationships through caring for one another. This extended even into the larger Greco-Roman society. They scattered outwardly to care for their poor, sick, and dying neighbors as they also cared for those within their beloved gathered community.[85] This caught the notice of emperor Julian who affirmed that Christians, "devoted themselves to philanthropy," cited Stark.[86]

Christianity revitalized life in Greco-Roman cities by providing new norms and new kinds of social relationships able to cope with many urgent urban problems. To cities filled with the homeless and impoverished, Christianity offered charity as well as hope. To cities filled with newcomers and strangers, Christianity offered an immediate basis for attachments. To cities filled with orphans and widows, Christianity provided a new

---

82   Ibid., pp. 12-17; 25.
83   Stark, *The Rise of Christianity*, p. 149.
84   Christine D. Pohl, *Making Room: Recovering Hospitality as a Christian Tradition*, (Grand Rapids, MI: William B. Eerdmans Publishing Company, 1999), p. 83.
85   Stark, *Rise of Christianity*, pp. 188-189.
86   Ibid., p. 189.

and expanded sense of family. To cities torn with violent strife, Christianity offered a new basis for social solidarity (cf. Pelikan 1987:21). And to cities faced with epidemics, fires, and earthquakes, Christianity offered effective nursing services.[87]

The Jesus Way was bound together by both the message they proclaimed and by the way they embodied that message. They had common spiritual practices which included a common way of life where love of neighbor was practiced *with* community and *in* the community, contributing to a sense of belonging.[88] In Rodney Stark's concluding reflection in *The Rise of Christianity*, he reiterates that his book's thesis was that the "central doctrines of Christianity prompted and sustained attractive, liberating, and effective social relations and organization."[89] Over and above that, states Stark, "it was the *way* these doctrines *took on flesh*, the way they directed organizational actions and individual behavior that led to the rise of Christianity (emphases mine)."[90] With regard to the proclamation, what was new and revolutionary about the Christian movement was the truth that God *loves* humanity, and that precisely because of that reality, their love for one another "must extend beyond the boundaries of family and tribe" to even beyond the Christian community itself.[91] Remarkably, the Jesus Way served as a "revitalization movement within the empire" where all were welcome in the midst of cultural chaos.[92] The gathering and scattering movement of the Jesus Way liberated social relations between the genders, within the family, and modulated class differences in society.[93] In a world ruled by violence and domination, the Jesus Way demonstrated a new way to be human. The new humanity offered prophetic dissent to the dominant culture of society.[94]

---

87 Stark, *Rise of Christianity*, p. 161.
88 Sittser, *Water from a Deep Well*, pp. 50-68.
89 Stark, *Rise of Christianity*, p. 211.
90 Ibid.
91 Ibid., p. 212.
92 Ibid., p. 213.
93 Ibid., p. 214.
94 Brueggemann, *The Prophetic Imagination*, pp. 3-4. Brueggemann asserts that "the task of prophetic ministry is to nurture, nourish, and evoke a consciousness and perception alternative to the consciousness and perception of the dominant culture around us." (p. 3) Historically, the dominant

Gradually, in the late second and third centuries CE, the Church's institutionalization began to mirror Roman political organization with Cyprian and appointed bishops inspiring its new supervisory hierarchy of authority. The church began uniting around doctrines with the bishop's role as guardian.[95] After the conversion of Constantine in the fourth century, the persecuted Jesus Way, which comprised scarcely 10% of the empire, became the state religion of Rome, so that Christians represented over 50% of the empire by 360 CE.[96] Luu puts forth that "with Constantine's conversion, the religion of the persecuted, powerless, and disenfranchised rapidly became a religion of the powerful and dominant."[97] Persecuted faith became a privileged faith as Christianity melded with Rome to build a Christian kingdom through war and conquest, whereby Constantine "transformed the Roman culture into a 'Christian culture'."[98]

Still a minority voice rose up, pointing back to the earlier Jesus Way, as a "protest against a decadent and overly institutionalized ecclesiastical body and a restatement of the gospel teaching to fit the changed conditions of the times."[99] The Desert Ammas and Abbas were a countermovement to the compromising worldliness of the church, resulting in a mass exodus of people who sought "beatitude in solitude."[100] According to Sittser, the desert saints practiced spiritual discipline (*ascesis*), "imperturbable calm" (*apatheia*), with the ultimate goal of inner transformation in the virtues of humility and love (*agape*) displayed through outward service and hospitality toward others, especially the poor. As they scattered

---

culture is "uncritical, cannot tolerate serious and fundamental criticism, and will go to great lengths to stop it." (p. 4) Through prophetic dissent, the dominant status quo is critiqued and disrupted. Prophetic ministry has the capacity to hold with tension that criticism while also becoming energized with hope for new, imaginative ways that reform and revitalize an alternative community. Prophetic dissent can both liberate those at the mercy of the dominant while also dismantling the mechanisms that maintain that domination.

95   Elizabeth Conde-Frazier, *Atando Cabos: Latinx Contributions to Theological Education* (Grand Rapids, MI: William B. Eerdmans Publishing Company, 2021), p. 41.

96   Stark, *Rise of Christianity*, p. 6.

97   Luu, *Jesus of the East*, p. 34.

98   Ibid.; See also Sittser, p. 80.

99   Thomas M. Gannon and George W. Traub, *The Desert and the City* (Chicago: Loyola University Press, 1969), p. 23.

100   Gonzalez, *The Story of Christianity*, p. 137.

out into the margins of society, they "challenged, comforted, and served the mainstream."[101] Communal gatherings formed as a corrective to the extremity of solitude. They were relational groups, primarily separated by gender, gathering to listen to instruction, to receive the sacraments, and to pray.[102] They called back to the "ways of the Jesus Way"—of earlier times while still pointing forward to the future kingdom of God to come. In this way, they were a prophetic minority voice of dissent.[103]

Brueggemann explains that both in scripture and in culture, the minority voice beckons attention and is prophetic. Though marginalized and suffering, this voice reveals the transcendent voice of God to penetrate "the numbness of history."[104] Subversively, these minority voices speak truth to power, refusing to accept the majority expressions as authentic. The prophetic lament from the margins is honest yearning, and from within it, God's voice of co-suffering love is expressed.[105] Flood reiterates that "by listening to these minority voices, speaking from the margins—giving voice to the victims of religious scapegoating violence—that we can become aware of how our own interpretations and theology, intended for good, can become hurtful. When we can learn to hear these protests from the margins this leads us to reform and compassion.[106] The Jesus Way of love for God and love for neighbor is re-expressed, revitalized, and reimagined as God's voice speaking from the margins beckons his people to return to their first love—to love first. This prophetic message is a spiritual and formational embodiment of protest displayed communally on the margins in a given generation.

According to Bass, the prophetic tradition discomforts the mainstream community, and awakens it to see injustices in its midst, urging it "to more fully embody God's dream of healing and love for all peo-

---

101 Sittser, *Water from a Deep Well,* pp. 80-93.
102 Ibid., p. 87.
103 Brueggemann, *The Prophetic Imagination,* p. 36.
104 Ibid., p. 55
105 Ibid. p. 65.
106 Derek Flood, *Disarming Scripture: Cherry-picking Liberals, Violence-loving Conservatives, and Why We All need to Learn to Read the Bible Like Jesus Did* (San Francisco: Metanoia Books, 2014), p. 99.

ples."[107] Institutions tend toward the pastoral role of comforting, sharing values, and reinforcing traditions. Institutions are slow and resistant to change—and resistant to prophets. On the other hand, prophets agitate, question, push for change and for "people to behave better toward one another."[108] Bass summarizes the historical Christian movement as a story which holds a tension between order and prophecy. "Jesus came as a prophet, one who challenged and transformed Judaism. A charismatic community grew up around his teachings and eventually formed into the church. The church organized, and then became an institution."[109] The institution guides and provides meaning for people while also guarding and protecting its power, wealth, and influence. The prophetic minority notices that the institutional ways have become discordant with God's ways and so they become discontent and question these conventional ways; experiment with new ideas and spiritual practices; and draw attention to those who are oppressed or excluded by the institution. Breaking institutional rules, the prophetic margins challenge the church.[110] Bass elaborates about the effects of this pattern. "The established church typically ignored them, sometimes tolerated them, often branded them heretics, tried to control them, and occasionally killed them. When enough people joined the ranks of the discontented, the institutional church had to pay attention. In the process, and sometimes unintentionally, the church opened itself up for genuine change and renewal."[111]

In addition to the monastic response of the desert saints in the fourth and fifth centuries, many other prophetic movements of discontent burst out of the boundaries of religious institutions to flow outward, creating various new forms along the margins in Christian history. Some of these communal movements of embodied prophetic dissent include: Gerhard Groote's Brothers and Sisters of the Common Life in the fourteenth cen-

---

107 Bass, *Christianity After Religion*, p. 88.
108 Ibid., p. 89.
109 Ibid.
110 Ibid.
111 Ibid.

tury;[112]Count Zinzendorf's Herrnhut community in the eighteenth century;[113] Dietrich Bonhoeffer's underground seminary, Finkenwalde, in the twentieth century;[114] and the emergent New Monasticism movement in the twenty-first century.[115] Many such movements evolved locally or organically or were unnamed and short-lived, yet their influence lives on in history books.[116]

A cursory examination of these and other prophetically dissenting groups reveals a renewal, reform, or revival of one or more of the fourfold spiritual practices in Acts 2:42-47. These practices characterized the early

---

112 Gonzalez, *The Story of Christianity*, (vol. 1), pp. 358-359; Sittser, *Water From a Deep Well*, pp. 202-204; Roger Olson, *The Story of Christian Theology: Twenty Centuries of Tradition and Reform* (Downers Grove, IL: IVP Academic, 1999), pp. 361, 375. In contrast with monastic orders, Brothers and Sisters of the Common Life were laypeople who maintained secular vocations, lived in community, shared their income, and followed contemplative devotional principles centered on imitating the life of Christ. They created educational centers to combat worldly Church corruption to effectually renew and reform the church. Notably, this group influenced Martin Luther and Erasmus.

113 Gonzalez, *The Story of Christianity*, (vol. 2), pp. 208-209; Sittser, *Water from a Deep Well*, pp. 243-244; Olson, *The Story of Christian Theology*, pp. 482-490. Hussites fleeing persecution as refugees from Moravia sought asylum to form an inclusive community of Catholics, Anabaptists, Lutherans, and separatists at Herrnhut. They banded together for prayer, scripture study, and song-filled "love feasts" with a non-doctrinal emphasis for experiencing intimate love with Jesus as motivation to scatter abroad to preach the gospel and serve the needy. John Wesley was deeply impacted by this movement.

114 Sittser, *Water from a Deep Well*, p. 69; Bonhoeffer, *Life Together*, pp. 1-122; William Samson, "The Finkenwalde Project," *Monasticism Old and New* (Waco, TX: The Center for Christian Ethics, 2010), pp. 19-25. Refusing to compromise as a German Christian in Nazi Germany, Bonhoeffer formed an underground monastic seminary, Finkenwalde, calling back to communal "life together," contemplative prayer rhythms, singing spiritual songs, and the study of the Sermon on the Mount to integrate heart, mind and action. Bonhoeffer prophesied a "new monasticism" for living the Sermon on the Mount ethics in the real world. The emergent New Monastic movement was seeded by Bonhoeffer's prophetic vision.

115 Samson, "Finkenwalde Project," pp. 22-25; Bass, "Bringing It To Completion: American New Monastics and the Benedictine Tradition," pp. 352-363; James Ponzetti, Jr. "Renewal in Catholic Community Life and New Monasticism: The Way of a Contemporary Religious Communal Movement," *The Journal for the Sociological Integration of Religion and Society* 4, no.2 (Fall 2014): pp. 35-50. The emergence of the New Monastic Movement joined various denominational traditions to form quasi-monastic intentional communities motivated to engage contemporary social injustices while adopting monastic rules of life in urban settings. Right belief with right practice through nonviolent activism, inclusivity, and reconciliatory practice is emphasized. Prominent leaders include Shane Claiborne (Simple Way Community) and Jonathan Wilson-Hartgrove (Rutba House).

116 Bass, *Christianity After Religion*, pp. 90-91.

gatherings of the Jesus Way but had been neglected or lost by the institutional church in the cultural moment of that time period. Resurgences of this common life were repeatedly embodied and expressed experientially in these groups and through their care for the poor and oppressed people in society in their day. In other words, prophetic dissenters centered the Jesus Way of love for God and for neighbors in the beloved community as the embodied expression of the kingdom of God.

Although an in-depth study of this pattern of tension between order and prophecy is beyond the scope of this book, the pattern manifests and persists in various cultural forms throughout Christian history. The forward, revitalizing momentum of scattering and gathering that occurred because of this tension should also be acknowledged. Optimally, a symbiosis of order and prophecy emerges—as in the earliest spirit-led "ways of the Jesus Way." A mutual regard for the interdependence of pastoral order and prophetic dissent in institutional and organic expressions of the Jesus Way is a "re-membering" that points toward the future restoration of all things. This is how an embodied spirituality is re-membered, re-formed and actively working to restore love for God and love of neighbor in the socio-cultural milieu of the present generation.

CHAPTER 3

PANDEMIC PAUSE

A Time to Scatter and a Time to Gather

CE, not AD, or BC

Pandemics change history.[117] In the liminal space of the COVID-19 global pandemic, Stark's insights on the impact of epidemics and the early Christian response to them help us grapple with similar theological questions. During the rise of the early Church in the Roman Empire, a fifteen year epidemic (suspected to be smallpox) in 165 CE killed at least one-quarter to one-third of the empire's population.[118] In 251 CE another epidemic (suspected to be measles) devastated the empire again, significantly depopulating it.[119] Stark quotes epidemic historian, Zinsser, who stated that "the forward march of Roman power and world organization was interrupted by the only force against which political genius and military valor were utterly helpless—epidemic disease..."[120] Zinsser linked the disruptive and demoralizing impact of epidemics with the Empire's decline. Stark asserts that while the epidemics were unexplainable and inconsolable under pagan and Hellenistic philosophies, Christianity offered a more hopeful theodicy as it embodied Christian love by "social service and community solidarity" as Jesus followers selflessly cared for the sick and dying.[121] With the rise of Christianity came "the linking of a high *social* ethical code with

---

117 Amanda Onion, Missy Sullivan, and Matt Mullen (eds.), "Pandemics that Changed History," www.history.com
(December 21, 2021); available online: https://www.history.com/topics/middle-ages/pandemics-timeline; accessed January 20, 2022
118 Stark, *The Rise of Christianity*, p. 73.
119 Ibid.
120 Hans Zinsser quoted in Stark, *The Rise of Christianity*, p. 74.
121 Ibid.

religion."[122] Stark continues, "Equally alien to paganism was the notion that because God loves humanity, Christians cannot please God unless they *love one another*. Indeed, as God demonstrates his love through sacrifice, humans must demonstrate their love through sacrifice on behalf of *one another*. Moreover, such responsibilities were to be extended beyond the bonds of family and tribe…"[123] Early Christians practiced these revolutionary and scriptural ideas demonstrating kenotic love through caring behavior in the midst of a culture in crisis. Their self-giving, co-suffering love for and with neighbors and enemies alike displayed the self-giving, co-suffering, cruciform love of their God in action. Their loving actions unveiled the Way.

Likewise, crises in the natural or social spheres of society frequently precipitate crises of *faith* throughout history, says Stark. In times of societal crises, the faith tradition may fail "to provide a satisfactory explanation of *why* the disaster occurred" and it "may seem to be *unavailing* against the disaster."[124] Ambiguous loss—this collective "frozen grief"—initiates questions of theodicy.[125] In a news article from December 31, 2021 concerning the effects of the COVID-19 pandemic on organized religion, one millennial generation leader stated, "Some of the things that we're told in traditional religion don't seem logical or rational…So people are leaving…but humans still have the same questions: Is there meaning or purpose in our existence? Why do we suffer?"[126] Over two years of a 'worldwide state of perpetual crisis' induced by the pandemic—further compounded by collective trauma from race-driven social unrest, polit-

---

122 Ibid., p. 86.
123 Ibid.
124 Ibid., p. 77.
125 Pauline Boss, *Ambiguous Loss: Learning to Live With Unresolved Grief* (Cambridge, MA: Harvard University Press, 1999), pp. 1-7. Boss describes the devastation of ambiguous loss because it remains "unclear, indeterminate." Although people yearn for certainty, ambiguous loss seems unending, absurd, ungraspable, as if frozen in time and space. Most certainly, the experience of global pandemic is an experience of ambiguous loss.
126 Seema Mody, "Millennials Lead Shift Away from Organized Religion as Pandemic Tests Americans' Faith," www.cnbc.com December 31, 2021; available online: https://www.cnbc.com/2021/12/29/millennials-lead-shift-away-from-organized-religion-as-pandemic-tests-faith.html; accessed January 20, 2022.

ical strife, economic recession, and natural disasters—creates the perfect storm for faith deconstruction.[127]

Within the context of epidemics, Stark attests to a concurrent phenomenon that percolates alongside times of societal crisis. "Revitalization movements" arise as a response to natural and social crises, especially within societal frameworks of rapid modernization and technological advances.[128] The way religions revitalize is through "effectively mobilizing people to attempt collective actions."[129] This increases the culture's capacity for positive problem-solving because "new ideas or theologies often generate new social arrangements that are better suited to the new circumstances."[130] Perhaps providentially, a diverse group of scholars gathered for "critical, theological conversations about the meanings and purposes of theological education in a time of deep change." The result of this collaborative project was to publish, between 2020-2022, the *Theological Education Between the Times* book series, to revitalize the Christian faith for future theological institutions and churches.[131] A brief scholarly analysis of themes in these books affecting spiritual formation will serve here to examine possibilities for the Jesus Way of the future, since theological institutions are a primary venue for the training of future pastors and faith leaders.

---

127 Marisa Iati, "The Pandemic Has Caused Nearly Two Years of Collective Trauma. Many People Are Near a Breaking Point," *Washington Post,* December 24, 2021, available online: https://www.washingtonpost.com/health/2021/12/24/collective-trauma-public-outbursts/;accessed January 20, 2022.
128 Stark, *The Rise of Christianity,* p. 78.
129 Ibid.
130 Ibid., p. 79.; Gonzalez, *The Story of Christianity,* p. 328. This seems to be true during medieval history as well where the bubonic plague devastated European economics, creating political turmoil, riots and social instability with religious consequences. Gonzalez relates that "it seemed that the Death had come to prefer younger victims" since the majority of victims were the healthy and the young. This was paradoxical with their cultural ideas about a "rationally ordered universe" which led to doubt, superstition and an obsession with death, "since death was always at the threshold."; Sittser, *Water from a Deep Well,* p. 166. Similarly, Sittser relates that the height of Christian mysticism was during the Middle Ages, stating that "mystics relish paradox." As the bubonic plague raged throughout Europe, mysticism "found a way to explain its vision of spiritual reality to the larger church, though often with a quiet voice."
131 Smith, *Theological Education Between the Times Book Series,* quote from inside the series' book covers.

Associate professor of systematic theology and Africana studies at Yale University Divinity School, Willie James Jennings, asserts that the central work of theological education is formational,[132] cultivating belonging.[133] To facilitate this work, distortions produced by whiteness must be addressed and boundaries transgressed to shift away from hegemony.[134] When gatherings break barriers and borders to draw people toward each other with intimacy, mutuality, and deeper interconnectedness, spiritual formation through communion is possible.[135] Theological education about belonging envisions communal "exchange networks" that are informed by stories told by nonwhite peoples and must be characterized by a willingness to be changed through instruction by non-white people.[136]

Through the lens of the traumatic history of colonization among Latin American people, nationally recognized authority on Hispanic Bible Institutes, Elizabeth Conde-Frazier, foresees a Holy-Spirit-centered decolonized paradigm for interpreting scripture as a means by which theological education can integrate theology and practice in broader faith communities.[137] This process is communal, collaborative, and testimonial; the theologians reside within the local community itself.[138] Contemplation in the present moment poses relevant questions to the biblical text, within the community's lived realities, or *viviencias*.[139] New spaces for theological reflection that are more mobile, virtual, and mystical will open up expressions through which social justice and trauma healing are offered to the suffering local community.[140]

Associate professor of constructive theology and African American religion at Princeton Theological Seminary, Keri Day, offers a prophetic critique of institutional theological spaces written as a testimonial about

---

132 Willie James Jennings, *After Whiteness: An Education in Belonging* (Grand Rapids, MI: William B. Eerdmans Publishing Company, 2020), pp. 4-6.
133 Ibid., pp 10-12.
134 Ibid., pp. 6-7.
135 Ibid., pp. 13-20; 129
136 Ibid., pp. 138-155.
137 Conde-Frazier, *Atando Cabos*, pp. 114-119.
138 Ibid. p. 128.
139 Ibid., pp. 114-116.
140 Ibid., p. 117.

how these spaces are experienced by "those from the underside of American society."[141] She centralizes the voices of those marginalized by race and ethnicity in order to imagine more open, creative and life-giving spaces that are embodied, artistic, and communal to join stories that are different together with questions and deep listening.[142] She describes a Pentecostal vision that unleashes miraculous disruptive power to defy the status quo driven by power differentials in society.[143] Day envisions an inclusive "theology of the edge" for the formation of radical communities of healing, love, and justice that moves across barriers of religion, class, gender, and class differences in local contexts.[144]

Notable Pentecostal theologian at Fuller Theological Seminary, Amos Yong, observes that globally, and most rapidly in the Global South, Christianity flourishes where a Pentecostal and charismatic movement prevails. This suggests the necessity of a robust pneumatology in belief and praxis as a priority for theological education.[145] A spirit-filled education must be reimagined both ecumenically and globally, to connect and network with greater accessibility in a "glocal" public square at a grassroots level.[146] Discussions about theological curriculum must highlight dialogical methods "with a genuine reciprocity of mutual discovery,"[147] not merely content and discourse. Yong's goal is "to understand church in its organic relationality and experiential spirituality," and to reimagine new forms of spirit-led theological education through multidimensional dialogue.[148]

As a prominent leader in the global Chinese Christian community and professor at Logos Evangelical Seminary, Chloe T. Sun relates that in light of globalization and the decline of Christianity in the West, diasporic communities of Chinese, Korean, and Hispanic students in theological

---

141 Keri Day, *Notes of a Native Daughter: Testifying in Theological Education* (Grand Rapids, MI: William B. Eerdmans Publishing Company, 2021), p. 1.
142 Ibid., pp.18; 25-27; 31
143 Ibid., pp. 15-17.
144 Ibis., pp. 34; 126-129.
145 Amos Yong, *Renewing the Church by the Spirit: Theological Education After Pentecost* (Grand Rapids, MI: William B. Eerdmans Publishing Company, 2020), pp. 28-32
146 Ibid., pp. 5-7; 22
147 Ibid., pp. 117; 108.
148 Ibid., p. 11.

institutions and churches in the West are rising exponentially.[149] This reality facilitates pluralistic theological constructs and practices as the center
of Christianity shifts from the minority world to the 2/3 majority world
of the Global South also present in the diverse diaspora in the West.[150] Mi-
gration of Christians to the West has a revitalizing effect through holistic
healing and church planting founded on formational prayer for bringing
scripture to life through the Holy Spirit—healing, reconciling, and restoring individuals and communities.[151] Sun stresses that effective theological
practices are contextual; spiritual formation takes place within a "hermeneutical community."[152] Language issues and cultural learning style
differences (i.e. virtue-oriented in contrast with mind-oriented) present
challenges to understanding each other. Contributions from the diaspora
include the formation of servants rather than leaders, gender role equality
in ministry, and theologies for suffering and persecution.[153]

Mark D. Jordan, professor of divinity at Harvard Divinity School,
does not offer solutions nor systems for best practices in theological instruction in his book, but instead suggests that "scenes of instruction"
are sheltered and shaped by time, encouraging embodied practice and
ethical training.[154] Jordan considers the variety of ways Jesus taught (parable, discussions, reframing rituals), to demonstrate creative approaches for
theological instruction.[155] Instruction must de-professionalize for spiritual
formation to take root and grow. A re-imagined instruction that animates
students will use story as a tool to reenact and inhabit theological truths
in ways that spiritually transforms their lives.[156] Scenes of instruction are
more difficult to imagine and activate in institutional settings. Jordan in-
cites experiments with teaching models for theology such as "apprentice-

---

149 Chloe T. Sun, *Attempt Great Things for God: Theological Education in Diaspora* (Grand Rapids, MI:
William B. Eerdmans Publishing Company, 2020), pp. 1-2.
150 Ibid., p. 2.
151 Ibid., pp. 20-28.
152 Ibid., pp. 37-40
153 Ibid., pp. 46, 56-59, 118
154 Jordan, *Transforming Fire*, pp. vii-viii.
155 Ibid., pp. 15-27.
156 Ibid., pp. 150-156.

ships, intentional communities, and houses of study alongside universities."[157]

As the executive director of the Association of Theological Schools for many years, Daniel O. Aleshire states that theological education embodies and moves forward religious impulses in the present cultural moment.[158] He cites current data depicting a declining positive view of the ethics of clergy by 20% over the last fifteen years and a declining confidence in organized religion of 30% from 1975-2018, to argue for the need of an educational model which stresses spiritual formation.[159] Spiritual formation practices include the time for cultivating character qualities, theological reflection, and moral sensitivity which goes beyond the acquisition of cognitive facts and tools.[160] In this way, the student becomes a "thinking, feeling, and acting being," with relational and behavioral authenticity and engagement with cultural relevance.[161] Mentors' beliefs and ethics must align as models for the next generation. Spiritual directors may serve as companions for younger people by facilitating spiritual growth and helping them cultivate skills for discernment on their spiritual journey.[162] Formational education must include a search for truth through reflective, communal questioning and the exercise of Christian virtues (i.e. humility, faith, self-denial, and charity) for spiritual and moral maturity with relational integrity in order to engage the present cultural moment with justice and mercy initiatives.[163]

As this group of scholars from diverse racial, ethnic, and language, denominational, and theological education backgrounds presents their perspectives for the future, we see common themes for the Jesus Way forward rise to the surface. Collectively, they did not significantly highlight the specific content of instruction as much as *a way of belonging,*

---

157 Ibid., pp. 155.
158 Daniel O. Aleshire, *Beyond Profession: The Next Future of Theological Education* (Grand Rapids, MI: William B. Eerdmans Publishing Company, 2021), pp. 2; 70-71.
159 Ibid, p. 77.
160 Ibid. p. 79.
161 Ibid., pp. 80; 83-90.
162 Ibid., pp. 105; 124.
163 Ibid., pp. 121-131.

being, and acting as learners—as disciples who follow the Spirit of Jesus.[164] Their commonalities inform a new approach for both faith leaders and grassroots laypeople. The following summaries synthesize these spiritually formational thematic threads woven into a tapestry for a future vision of the Jesus Way in the twenty-first century.

Belonging

Throughout the *Theological Education Between the Times* book series, words conveying the idea of "belonging" are found everywhere. The *way* forward is communal where there is relational connection, collaboration, a joining and a weaving of lives together. Optimally, gatherings are multidimensional. A rich blend of diverse marginalized voices with regard to race, ethnicity, language, gender, ability, and religious particularity are inclusively united with mutual regard to hold differences with respectful tension. This alternative community can disrupt existing power differentials as an alternative community within the culture. A community of bodies meeting together in local contexts provides a sense of belonging that is culturally relevant, authentic, and visible to neighbors. In the twenty-first century, communities may be further reimagined as online/virtual communities, exchange networks, intentional cohorts, mobile small groups, mystic/contemplative gatherings, and creative/artistic spaces to expand diversity and inclusion.

---

164 Diana Butler Bass, *Christianity After Religion*, pp. 103 – 198. Again, I am indebted to Bass' sequential categories of "belonging, believing, and behaving" from her prophetic book. A decade after its publishing, I have nuanced her vocabulary here to describe what her prophetic nomenclature has revealed as a manner of *being* (experiential and contemplative) to replace her designation of "believing" and *acting* (re-enacting of the ways of love through social justice and merciful actions) to replace "behaving" in order to avoid the dysphemism associating those words with "belief" as specific dogma/doctrine and "behave" with its drive for religious performance in this continuing cultural moment of faith deconstruction.

Being

Spiritual formation was the clarion call voiced by every author in the book series. Formation must be Spirit-led, Pentecostal, and communal so it remains fluid, miraculous and life-giving as the sacred text stories are decolonized for ongoing reenactment and reimagination. The scholars emphasize communal spiritual formation with shared facilitation and mutually reciprocal dialogue so that all voices are formative, and marginalized ones are centered. Holy Spirit approaches for decolonizing sacred texts involve localized hermeneutics with diverse voices amplified through storytelling, asking questions, reenacting narrative, and testimonials. Communal interpretation of sacred text together is prayerful and contemplative with deep listening together. The Holy Spirit hermeneutic leads to discovery as participants struggle together over time and across linguistic and cultural barriers within a given diasporic locale. In the relational process, through spiritually formative practices shaped by human diversity, hearts transform to develop virtues such as humility and charity, servanthood and endurance, through stories of cultural differences in experience, suffering and persecution. A local hermeneutic develops through multiple modes of instruction, shared stories, discussions, and rituals, and is further developed by a shared lived reality in which the scenes of instruction are sheltered and shaped by decolonized sacred texts. In addition to the renewed emphasis on communal transformation, individual spiritual formation with mature mentors and spiritual directors as companions facilitates spiritual maturity and virtue development through an apprenticeship model, aligning with the Jesus Way of life.

Acting

The integration (and not mere "balance") of theology with practice, orthodoxy with orthopraxy, was a common theme among authors in the *Theological Education Between The Times* book series. Aligning orthodoxy with orthopraxy must be practiced within the formational community itself and in the present cultural moment at large as an alternative way of living out faith in Jesus. Dialogue must take place with diverse voices to illuminate the gospel's glocal perspective with global reach. The orthodox truths enacted through social justice activism, mercy initiatives, and compassionate solidarity with the lived realities of suffering in our world speak truth to power, upending unjust systems that oppress people while mercifully offering healing through charitable embrace in action. This holistic *way* of belonging, being, and acting in the world offers collective trauma healing, restoration, and reconciliation for diverse people through the Spirit of Jesus transforming the world through the people of the Way.

During a cultural moment of global pandemic pause, these diverse theologians with a unified voice, cry out for a better way forward for the future of the church and its influence in the world for good. No doubt, a "revitalization movement" is stirring during the worldwide crisis. A decade ago, Diana Butler Bass prophesied a forthcoming new global Great Awakening. "This awakening is being performed in a networked world, where the border between the sacred and secular has eroded and where the love of God and neighbor—and the new vision of belonging, behaving, and believing—is being staged far beyond conventional religious communities."[165] Where do these non-conventional religious communities of the *Way* forward, already "live and move and have their being?"[166] We look along the margins, for the prophetic voices over the last 20 years to discover a more embodied, Christlike, Spirit-led, *contemplative* approach for belonging, being, and acting as the Jesus Way of the future.

---

165 Diana Butler Bass, *Christianity After Religion,* p. 258.
166 Acts 17:28.

CHAPTER 4

PREPARING THE WAY

Prophetic Dissenting Voices Today

In order to reveal the prophetic dissenting voices preparing the way as a revitalizing movement for our present generation, we look to the minority voices of those suffering ones in the margins, where Brueggemann says, the transcendent voice of God speaks.[167] Globally, the stereotypic view of Christianity as a Western religion that is "un-black, un-poor, and un-young" has shifted, sweeping through the massively diverse 2/3 majority world in the Global South and East among the most marginalized groups of people in the world, namely those living in Africa, Latin America, and Asia.[168] Jenkins relates, "If we want to visualize a 'typical' contemporary Christian, we should think of a woman living in a village in Nigeria, or in a Brazilian *favela*."[169] Jenkins describes this expansive 'world Christianity'

---

167 Walter Brueggemann, *The Prophetic Imagination*, p. 55.

168 Philip Jenkins, *The Next Christendom: The Coming of Global Christianity* (revised and expanded edition), (New York: Oxford University Press, 2007), pp. 1-3. See also, Elaine A. Heath, *The Mystic Way of Evangelism: A Contemplative Vision for Christian Outreach* (Grand Rapids, MI: Baker Academic, 2017), p. xi.

169 Ibid.; Jenkins extrapolates the statistics of Christian predominance in the Global South to project forward to 2025. "Assuming no great gains or losses through conversion, then there would be around 2.6 billion Christians, of whom 595 million would live in Africa, 623 million in Latin America, and 498 million in Asia. Europe, with 513 million, would have slipped to third place. Africa and Latin America would thus be in competition for the title of most Christian continent. About this date, too, another significant milestone should occur, namely that these two continents will together account for half the Christians on the planet. By 2050 only about one-fifth of the world's three billion Christians will be non-Hispanic whites. Soon the phrase "a white Christian" may sound like a curious oxymoron...," (p. 3). Obviously, these projections do not take into account the global disparities affecting mortality through the current COVID-19 pandemic.

as "more spontaneous and rooted in the lives of the (mainly poor) inhabitants."[170]

> African and Latin American Christians are people for whom the New Testament Beatitudes have a direct relevance inconceivable for most Christians in Northern societies. When Jesus told the "poor" they were blessed, the word used does not imply relative deprivation, it means total poverty, or destitution. The great majority of Southern Christians (and increasingly, of all Christians) really are the poor, the hungry, the persecuted, even the dehumanized.[171]

Jenkins' prophetic voice of dissent amplifies the reality of the global margins to de-center Western views about the peopling of the Jesus Way in the Third Millennium.

Furthermore, Jenkins describes the characteristics of Global South followers of Jesus. The way of embodiment for these followers has a strong supernatural orientation where "Pentecostal expansion across the Southern Continents [has been] so astonishing as to justify claims of a new Reformation."[172] Yong concurs with this "pentecostalization" and attributes this phenomenon to the expansion of "classical Pentecostal movements," charismatic renewal in traditional church institutions, and to "the character of indigenous Asian, African, and Latin American spiritualities that map rather effortlessly onto Pentecostal and charismatic sensibilities, practices, and inclinations."[173] Heath boldly asserts that Pentecostal forms of indigenous Christianity in the Global South bear little resemblance to North American Pentecostalism with its prosperity gospel messaging. This indigenous Pentecostalism does not frequently find its origin in the West

---

170 Ibid., p. xiii.
171 Ibid., p. 256.
172 Ibid., p. 8.
173 Yong, *Renewing the Church By the Spirit*, p. 29.

and is pan-denominational. It is characterized by an egalitarian leadership approach with teams representing the ethnicity, racial makeup, and economic social classes of the local context, with men and women "sharing equally in power, service and discernment."[174] In addition, there is a "flattening" of traditional ecclesiology that emphasizes lay participation through relational networks.[175]

Global South followers of Jesus take the Bible seriously; its words are engaged and embodied in local contexts. The Bible, with its supernatural signs and wonders highlighted in the New Testament narratives, supports indigenous worldviews based on spirits, miracles, healing, dreams, and deliverance. This ancient world described in its texts is relevant as a present reality among the marginalized in the Global South, with signs of the kingdom manifesting in the here and now, vividly pointing to the future kingdom.[176] "The vitality of prophecy in the contemporary South means that the rising churches can read biblical accounts with far more understanding and sensitivity than Northern Christians can. In the book of Acts, prophecy was a sign of the true church."[177]

Jenkins expounds that "In Southern Pentecostal and independent churches, though, belief goes much farther to the stage of participation in a present event."[178] As people enter into and participate in the stories of the Bible, the words of ancient texts parallel the world in which they live; these stories become contemporary, lived-out realities in their communal contexts.[179] The Bible's core social and political themes of oppression, exile, and persecution are relevant. "In the present day, it may be that it

---

174 Elaine A. Heath, *The Mystic Way of Evangelism: A Contemplative Vision for Christian Outreach,* (Grand Rapids, MI: Baker Academic, 2017), pp. 150-152.
175 Yong, *Renewing the Church by the Spirit,* p. 29.
176 Jenkins, *The Next Christendom,* pp. 148-149.
177 Ibid., p. 149.
178 Ibid., p. 148.
179 Jennings, *Acts,* pp. 2-3. Jennings explains the dynamic nature of storytelling as history unfolds in a future to help the present circumstances become understandable. He relates that the Spirit is present in the storytelling. Jennings elaborates, "God has entered the life of the creature and joined the storytelling that is history. Now the divine life may ride on multiple narrations of creatures. God has joined in the storytelling, as well, but with God a different procedure explodes on the scene. God plays in the telling, moving back and forth from past to present to future. There in the storytelling of the past, now in present storytelling and ready, anticipating future telling."

is only in the newer churches that the Bible can be read with any authenticity and immediacy, and that the Old Christendom must give priority to Southern voices."[180] Perhaps these suffering prophetic voices of the oppressed from the Global South can inform and direct the Western Church in caring for the suffering ones in our context who are oppressed because of race, ethnicity, ability and gender.

Undeniably, Christianity flourished among the poor and persecuted throughout history and now as evidenced in the Global South and the East in contrast with its diminishment among the rich and powerful in the West. "The evangelical and Pentecostal movements' cultural diversity and indigenous spiritualities" has a de-centering effect as these forms move through the networked diaspora in the contemporary "world Christianity."[181] A non-Western understanding of Christianity, as a "planetary phenomenon" is paramount for understanding what is emerging and re-forming faith today.[182] With the impact of globalization, the vision for revitalization goes beyond our myopic lens to the margins beyond our Western borders. Inclining our Western ears to hear the prophetic dissent crying out from the South and the East, the Spirit of Jesus transcends to speak prophetic truth to power in our day. Jenkins suggests that prophetic forecasts "more frequently do indeed happen but in forms quite different from what anyone expected."[183] A posture of intellectual humility is necessary to *learn from* these embodied expressions of spiritual formation as models for *theological* approaches for the future Western Church and its educational institutions.[184]

A glimpse into the most rapidly and organically growing, indigenous groups of Jesus followers in the Global South and East will serve as an

---

180 Jenkins, *The Next Christendom*, p. 257.

181 Ibid., p. 32. See also how this relates to the diaspora of the Global South "hybrid narratives" in the West in Sun, *Attempt Great Things*, p. 1-7.

182 Jenkins, *The Next Christendom*, p. 260.

183 Ibid. p. 251.

184 Michael J. Sandel, *The Tyranny of Merit: Can We Find the Common Good?* (New York: Picador, 2020), p. 97. Sandel asserts that "...at a time when racism and sexism are out of favor (discredited though not eliminated), credentialism is the last acceptable prejudice. In the United States and Europe, disdain for the poorly educated is more pronounced, or at least more readily acknowledged, than prejudice against other disfavored groups."

observation window through which to re-imagine a more Christlike, Spirit-led, contemplative approach for future gatherings of the Jesus Way in the West. Specifically, the phenomenon of rapid multiplication of organic gatherings of Jesus followers, referred to as Disciple-Making Movements (DMMs) will be examined. Like mustard seeds the kingdom of God has been deeply sown and rapidly spreading organically through Disciple Making Movements in the Global South and East over the last twenty years or more. What can we humbly learn about new ways for gathering and scattering from these enlivened kingdom forerunners to revitalize the collapsing, deconstructing Church in the West?

Cole defines the ideals of such disciple-making movements as "organic church."[185] "The core reality is not how the followers are organized, discipled, or helped. The core reality is Jesus Christ being followed, loved and obeyed. Christ alive, forming spiritual families and working with them to fulfill His mission, is the living reality of the organic church. The Church really is an embodiment of the risen Jesus. No wonder the Bible refers to the church as the Body of Christ."[186] Clear Christology, Cole states, leads to ecclesiology that bears fruit. Therefore, as followers connect people with the love of Jesus, they extend his reign on earth. Jesus builds the church and works through his gathered and scattered people. Jesus is the active Way, living *in* his beloved community and working *through* His Body to bring kingdom transformation to earthly people within their own cultural contexts. Seed is scattered in the culture's *indigenous* soil without Western constructs, and Christ's life flourishes and multiplies in their midst. The fruit of planting the good news of the kenotic love of Jesus as seeds is a transformed people living out their faith in Jesus together within their own culture's soil. Growth, reproduction, and sustenance in this rich, organic soil of love spreads, scattering seed by the wind of the Holy Spirit into new places to engage and transform cultures by bringing life and bearing more fruit.[187]

---

185 Neil Cole, "Organic Church," in *Perspectives on the World Christian Movement: A Reader*, 4th ed., eds. Ralph P. Winter and Steven C. Hawthorne (Pasadena, CA: William Carey Library, 2009), p. 645.

186 Ibid.

187 Ibid.; See also John 15:9-17.

Written over a century ago, Christoph Friedrich Blumhardt testifies to the spirit-led, organic nature of disciple-making in *Everyone Belongs to God.* Blumhardt believed with confidence that *all* the peoples of the earth belonged to God. Followers of Jesus were to *open* doors in life-giving ways to preach peace to all people.[188] In the introduction, Charles E. Moore explains Blumhardt's kingdom theology this way:

> Suffice it to say that the 'gospel of the Christians' has little or nothing to do with the revolutionary message of Christ itself. Jesus did not come to found churches, defined by doctrine or ritual, but to set in motion a movement of the Spirit that would encompass nations and lead to inner freedom, peace, and social justice. For Blumhardt, the 'gospel of Jesus Christ' has nothing to do with Christianity, Buddhism, or any other religion. "No longer religion against religion, but justice against sin, life against death."[189]

This hidden work of the Spirit works beneath the surface, subversively, through a practical, liberating love that draws all people to Jesus without coercion or manipulation. Followers of Jesus simply proclaim God's kingdom to all people. "God's kingdom *will* come," says Blumhardt.[190] He continues, "You must represent the living Christ who brings forth God's justice on the earth. Keep seeking God's kingdom in the love of Christ, and you will witness redemption in even the smallest matters. If you strive for God's justice in that name of all who suffer, not just for a few, redemption will come."[191] Blumhardt's timely words speak of the reality of

---

188 Christoph Friedrich Blumhardt, *Everyone Belongs to God: Discovering the Hidden Christ* (Walden, NY: Plough Publishing House, 2015), pp. ix – 9. This book is a collection of letters from Blumhardt, a famous pastor from 100 years ago, to his missionary son-in-law about "what it means to give witness to Christ." (from back cover).

189 Charles E. Moore, introduction to *Everyone Belongs to God: Discovering the Hidden Christ,* by Christoph Friedrich Blumhardt (Walden, NY: Plough Publishing House), p. xix.

190 Blumhardt, *Everyone Belongs to God,* pp. 1-9.

191 Ibid., p. 9.

a world of suffering and oppression, where God himself enters the misery of his people. Blumhardt's pithy admonition speaks a resounding word of hope today: "You belong to God!"[192] In simple proclamation and embodied practical love, "…With their own culture and language, they will be brought into the future unity of God's kingdom. For this reason, let the people develop at their own pace in economic and political matters, according to the times they live in. Whatever is necessary from God will come of itself, without our meddling."[193]

Jesus followers arise from this soil of neighborly love, reminiscent of the earlier Jesus Way in Acts. This spontaneous, organic movement of the Spirit continues today in DMMs in the Global South.[194] David Watson, global DMM strategist with Cityteam Ministries, recaps the story of how he learned from an elderly indigenous Jesus follower who was involved in a movement of the Spirit among the Bhojpuri people of North India. Sitting at his feet, Watson asked the elder to teach him his ways. He replied,

> It's not hard. Every morning my great niece reads to me from the Bible for one hour—I can't read so she reads for me. Then I think about what she read until lunch. I think about what it means and what God wants our family to do. When everyone comes in from the field for lunch, I tell them what God said through His Word to our family. Then I tell them to tell everyone they know what God said to our family that day. And they do. That's all. [195]

---

192 Ibid., p. 16.

193 Ibid., pp. 16-17.

194 David Garrison, "Church Planting Movements" in *Perspectives on the World Christian Movement: A Reader*, 4th ed., eds. Ralph D. Winter and Steven C. Hawthorne (Pasadena, CA: William Carey Library, 2009), p. 646-647.; Some, like Garrison, refer to these "rapid multiplication of indigenous churches planting churches that sweeps through a people group or population segment" as a Church Planting Movements (CPM). Others (including myself here) refer to the phenomenon as a Disciple Making Movements (DMM). For an explanation of the differentiation between a CPM and DMM, see David L. Watson and Paul D. Watson, *Contagious Disciple Making: Leading Others on a Journey of Discovery* (Nashville, TN: Thomas Nelson, 2014), pp. 3-7.

195 David L. Watson and Paul D. Watson, "A Movement of God Among the Bhojpuri of North India," in *Perspectives on the World Christian Movement: A Reader*, 4th ed., eds. Ralph D. Winter and Steven

Clearly, this simple testimony of spiritual formation is rich with wisdom. It expresses the humble, listening posture of a learner, with ears to hear the words of scripture. It demonstrates a slow, contemplative unfolding of truth through meditation with prayerful questions for God about how to act upon those words of truth in the world. There is communal sharing—testimony—over a meal with the family gathering to break bread while remembering God. Then more storytelling and testimony to reenact the story of God in real life with others that is simply good news for all people: we all belong to God!

The approach for engaging scripture described by the elderly Bhojpuri man to Watson is similar to what Brueggemann relates as "'doing the text' again, as our text and as 'news' addressed to us and waiting to be received, appropriated, and enacted in our own time and place."[196] The textual drama is imagined, participated in and reenacted. Brueggemann continues,

> The texts continue to be alive and invitational because they refuse to stay "back there," but always insist upon being "present tense" and contemporary. Thus biblical texts were not simply formed and fixed (either by some once-for-all divine disclosure or by some nameable human author); they were shaped by and for repeated use in the community, especially in the practice of worship, but in many other contexts as well.[197]

The stories of scripture, and their communal embodiment, become the way through which "all things are made new."[198] People are invited into a "counter-conversation" found in the pages of scripture.[199] As the liberating claims of Jesus are linked with tangible, practical love for neighbors, once again, "word here becomes flesh, sovereignty becomes

---

C. Hawthorne (Pasadena, CA: William Carey Library, 2009), p. 699.

196 Brueggemann, *Biblical Perspectives of Evangelism*, p. 8.
197 Ibid.
198 Ibid., p. 11.
199 Ibid., p. 43.

compassion, weakness becomes strength, foolishness becomes wisdom, suffering becomes hope, vulnerability becomes energy, death becomes life."[200] Embodying these transformations in local cultural contexts, disrupts, subverts, and transforms communities in the ways of the kingdom, enacting justice, peace, and a radical love reminiscent of earlier revitalizing expressions of the Jesus Way in the margins.

One accessible and reproducible approach for the communal instruction around scripture that is widely used in DMMs by practitioners like Watson is Discovery Bible Study (DBS).[201] Several models of Discovery Bible Studies exist, but I will be referencing the one found in Appendix A.[202] Discovery Bible Studies are essentially communal, and at their onset they engage existing social groupings so that cultural barriers are reduced. Since hospitality is valued in many cultures around the world, meetings often include the sharing of food and drinks in the context of homes; gatherings are typically small. Each Discovery Bible Study begins with personal storytelling open to everyone. Everyone shares what they are thankful for, what is causing stress, and how they can lovingly help each other or others in their community together. Eventually, as people recognize the Holy Spirit's presence in their midst, these stories of thanksgiving, suffering, and need are turned into prayer.[203]

Typically, Discovery Bible Studies are started by an outsider who serves as a facilitator. A facilitator does *not* teach, at least in typical ways, but facilitates discovery through asking questions. Facilitators are not the "answer-people," but instead point to the Holy Spirit as Teacher, encourage a listening posture as scripture is read, and invite the full participation and contributions of each member of the group for understanding texts. The story from scripture is retold by group members, a reenactment from within their cultural context. Others in the group contribute missing parts of the story they thought were important. The scripture is read

---

200 Ibid., p. 47.
201 Watson and Watson, *Contagious Disciplemaking*, pp. 144-154.
202 Discovery Bible Study Guide (pdf) on "Discovery Bible Study: A Safe Place to See for Yourself What the Bible Says," available online: https://www.dbsguide.org; accessed January 28, 2022. See also https://www.contagiousdisciplemakingcom; accessed January 28, 2022.
203 Watson and Watson, *Contagious Disciplemaking*, pp. 143-145; 152-153. See also Appendix A.

and reflected upon several times with simple question prompts. The Holy Spirit reveals the "good news for all people" through the scripture texts as people participate together in wrestling through questions about God and about people, primarily through the narrative stories of scripture.[204]

Participants receive spiritual understanding communally in the context of their own culture and language, because they are the ones who receive and offer their understanding of texts as the Spirit lovingly reveals transformative truths to their hearts. Every participant is both learner and teacher. The group is invited to follow Jesus through life-giving obedience, in their personal lives and out in their community, expressed and embodied from within their own socio-cultural particularity. The stories are retold to family, friends, and neighbors in their community until they meet again.[205]

As the stories of Jesus are retold in the community, social circles intersect, converge, and multiply through everyday disciples who can reach others outside of their original socio-cultural circles. Disciples make disciples and begin to interconnect with outsiders because of the presence of "persons of peace."[206] Watson says, "God has prepared men and women in every culture who can meet those who love Jesus from another culture, [and] learn to love Jesus from them..."[207] These "persons of peace" are relationally open, spiritually hungry, and readily share with others.[208] As the Spirit moves through people sharing stories of good news while embodying the Great Commandment of love for God and neighbor in their communities, the kingdom gospel of peace and justice manifests through individual lives and their communities in transformational, de-colonized ways. Though seemingly miniscule, these gatherings of followers scatter kingdom mustard seeds in indigenous soil that sprout and grow and spread miraculously to manifest a Disciple Making Movement.[209]

---

204 Ibid., pp. 143-153. See also Appendix A.
205 Ibid., pp. 141-154. See also Appendix A.
206 Ibid., pp. 123-125.
207 Ibid., p. 13.
208 Ibid., p. 135.
209 Ibid., pp. 190-200; Mark 4:26-34. See also, Jerry Trousdale, *Miraculous Movements.* (Nashville, TN: Thomas Nelson, 2012), p. 16.

From the grassroots perspective of Disciple Making Movements in the Global South and East, the Discovery Bible Study approach to gathering around scripture shares many of the features for future spiritual formation voiced by the scholarly authors in the *Theological Education Between the Times Series*. In these indigenous gatherings of the Global South and East, there is a culture of *belonging* expressed through authentic, relational connection in the context of community with a shared rhythm of life centered around scripture. As social circles of influence mobilize and converge, diversity naturally occurs among groups as the good news is spread. Their ways of *being* together include storytelling with egalitarian participation around the contemplative reading of scripture after reflecting on questions with deep listening. Since the Holy Spirit is Teacher, meaningful discoveries are spirit-led and revealed within their socio-cultural framework, and therefore, decolonized. What is being revealed through scripture is not only internalized for personal transformation but a way of *acting* in the world as the Jesus Way is followed in embodied expressions of peace, justice, and mercy with neighbors who need help and some good news to bring hope, faith, and love in the midst of their suffering.

Has the Church of the Global South and East paved the way as a prophetic forerunner for an approach for spiritual formation that will revitalize the Western Church? Is this a calling back in remembrance to the earlier "ways of the Jesus Way" throughout church history that might revitalize the institutional church? Does this way authentically embody and express the hope of a future kingdom of peace and justice when all will be restored?

Perhaps the answer is not so simple. At first glance, there are the obvious questions with such an approach. What if the scriptures are obeyed literally, especially the terrifying texts of violence? Is a human teacher (other than the Holy Spirit) needed to make sure that scriptures are not taken out of context? With all of our racial, ethnic, and gender divides, is it even possible to create a Christian community among people who are not only marginalized by society, but marginalized by the church itself? Possible solutions for addressing these questions can be found by listening to a few significant prophetic voices along the "edges" of contemporary theology. These voices have been orienteering ancient spiritual pathways for historically grounded formational practices which may offer nuanced solutions to some of these problems. Their reorienting ideas might lead to a more Christlike, Spirit-led, contemplative approach for reading scripture with diverse neighbors and an embodied love-ethic, pointing to a possible Jesus Way forward for our Third Millennium.

CHAPTER 5

PAVING THE WAY

Ancient-Future Orienteering with Spiritual Practices

If the disciple-making movement of the Global South and East prophet-ically speaks northward and westward to revitalize spiritual formation in our contexts, its gatherings should also display historically rooted spiritual practices that have defined the Jesus Way in the past. It is not a stretch to see that the Discovery Bible Study approach can encompass the fourfold spiritual practices of the early church gatherings in Acts 2:42-47: "the apostles' teaching; the common life of those who believed; the breaking of the bread; and the prayers." However, the *value* of ancient spiritual practices must be recovered for an outwardly expressed love-ethic that displays the resurrected Body of Christ bringing love, peace, and justice to the world. Renewing these ancient practices will enable the Jesus Way to develop a more apostolic hermeneutic for reading scripture; a more contemplative posture for prayer; and a more hospitable common life where Jesus is revealed in the "breaking of the bread." The Jesus Way of the future must be anchored in history in order to move forward with our authentic particularity as Jesus followers.

Drawing on "the power of our faith from God's unrelenting reach-ing out to people," Jesus followers hold on to hope for reconciliation among diverse people based on Christ's new commandment of love.[210] Throughout scripture, Moyaert contends, God reveals himself incognito in the form of the stranger. God first conceals and then reveals himself in someone who is utterly different from us in race, culture, language, and

---

210 Moyaert, *Fragile Identities: Towards a Theology of Interreligious Hospitality* (New York: Rodopi, 2011), p. 260.

religion. In our stranger's face, we see the image of God unfold. Through our stranger's story, our prejudices against the stranger, and consequently against God, are disrupted.[211] Moyaert explains that the Spirit of Truth warns against "claims of domination" not by removing differences but by making them accessible through the interruption of prejudices, making it possible to understand one another, despite our human fragility.[212] Jesus provides the example that we can receive the stranger freely and with trust because that is precisely where he reveals himself through the Spirit.[213] "Love is the new commandment given by Christ and it is this commandment that commands us to allow not brokenness but the eschatological hope of solidarity to prevail already now."[214] Who might be considered the "stranger" in our communities in the West today? We look again to the margins.

Those people living on the edges of Western society include "persons who are recovering from substance abuse, in therapy, undocumented, physically and emotionally disabled, recently incarcerated, living with HIV/AIDS, same gender loving (SGL) persons, transgendered persons."[215] Our BILPOC neighbors, refugees, immigrants from the diaspora, and those pushed to the edges because of their particular religious adherence are also disproportionately marginalized and stigmatized. Among the poorest and most isolated in Western communities are elderly neighbors and people living without housing.

This list is not exhaustive. In any given local context, disparities in race, gender, ethnicity, class, ability, resources, and opportunities abound, and so does the resulting stigmatization and marginalization associated with those disparities. Identifying with empathy and solidarity to learn from the "least of these"[216]—true humility—must be the essential posture for followers for a new Jesus Way forward that carries the aroma of Jesus who, with love and compassion, blesses those who are poor, mourning,

211 Ibid., pp, 260-266.
212 Ibid., p, 267.
213 Ibid., pp. 265; 271.
214 Ibid., p. 260.
215 Flunder, *Where the Edge Gathers*, p. xi.
216 Matthew 25: 45.

meek, hungry, thirsty, and persecuted. Those blessed ones, and those who stand in solidarity with these neighbors, are the merciful, the pure-hearted, the peacemaking prophets who are blessed with the "least of these."[217]

Jennings states that true disciples of Jesus Christ surprise the segregated world because they demonstrate intimacy in life together that transgresses boundaries and borders by inviting strangers into a new common life. He continues,

> Disciples connect peoples at sites of segregation, inviting a mutual enfolding of story within story: the stories of people enfolded in the story of God's love found in the resurrected Jesus and the stories of people enfolded in one another. This is precisely how a people's story may be carried into a flourishing future—by love for them found in others, and by others sharing with them in story, hope, and life. Indeed this work of the Spirit gifts us to one another as life partners, sharing in a common hope in the resurrection through Jesus Christ.[218]

Jennings prophesies that in our present moment, the church can no longer ignore the intentional work of the Spirit that is "pressing us to join with people we do not want to join with or imagine intimate life with."[219] What would it look like for this to be our spiritual formation goal together—to form a common life "where the struggle for justice meets radical hospitality and where people from every walk of life wander into a space filled with hope surprise, and very good news"?[220]

---

217 Matthew 5: 3-12; Matthew 25: 45.
218 Jennings, *Acts*, pp. 255-256.
219 Ibid., p. 255.
220 Ibid., p. 257.

Ancient-Future Spiritual Practices of Belonging: A Common Life and the Breaking of Bread

The archetype for the spiritual practice of the common life was enfleshed by the gatherings of the early church in Acts.[221] "Early Christian writers claimed that transcending social and ethnic differences by sharing meals, homes, and worship with persons of different backgrounds was a proof of the truth of the Christian faith."[222] They were to welcome each other as Christ welcomed them, and by hospitably welcoming the poor into their homes, "they would have Christ as their guest."[223] Wirzba explains that this welcoming, hospitable posture was reflective of the perichoretic communion of the Father, Son, and Spirit who "exist *with* each other in radical equality and unity"—a communion in which there is no subordination nor hierarchy.[224] Though distinct from each other, the Trinity shares life with complete, abiding, mutuality where each "makes room" *in* itself for the other.[225] Followers of Jesus who gather in this way participate in God's self-giving love, making room to be and to flourish in God's abundant life by mutually sharing themselves and their resources with self-giving love for neighbor. In this way the common life is spiritually formational, embodied and practical. Wirzba continues, "In other words, mutual indwelling, the other-in-me and myself-in-another, is at the heart of true reality. True life is lived *through* the gifts of others."[226] The common life shapes us, interweaving people "through expanding a sense of belonging in the Spirit-filled action of joining."[227] The common life provides a new orientation created by the Spirit who joins unlikely people with reciprocity.[228] Historic Christianity holds high God's desire that common life is a hospitable community of radical inclusion—a round, accessible, open

---

221 See Acts 2: 42-47; Acts 4: 32-37.
222 Pohl, *Making Room*, p. 5.
223 Ibid.
224 Norman Wirzba, *Food and Faith: A Theology of Eating*, 2nd ed. (Cambridge, UK: Cambridge University Press, 2020), pp. 48-49.
225 Ibid.
226 Ibid.
227 Jennings, *Acts,* p. 254.
228 Ibid., p. 39.

table where *all* are invited and "welcome to taste and see that God is good and merciful and a lover of humanity."[229]

Yvette A. Flunder's extensive inner-city pastoral experience with marginalized people in San Francisco frames her passion for "creating, sustaining, and celebrating Christian community among people who are marginalized by church and society and cannot or choose not to hide the cause of their marginalization."[230] She asserts that because of the visibility of the marginalizing characteristic (i.e., people of color, transgendered persons, persons with certain disabilities etc.), they are therefore vulnerable and "cannot hide their otherness in the dominant society."[231] A common life in the twenty-first century, that is true to its historic roots as the Jesus Way will strive to visibly join the "other-in-me" and "myself-in-another" to offer a place for healing so that "marginalized people [can] take back the right to fully 'be'."[232] Just as Jesus openly received the people most oppressed by society and religion, our common life together must "reach from the center to the farthest margin and work its way back."[233] We reach for those who are the least accepted ones—"the least of these"—authentically, inclusively, and with radical love.[234]

Flunder develops her "Twelve Steps: The Refuge Radical Inclusivity Model"[235] to flesh out what a common life must recover to follow Jesus' model of radical love in community on the margin. Radical inclusivity reaches out to the farthest margin, welcoming everyone. It "recognizes, values, loves, and celebrates people on the margin."[236] It recognizes the real harm done in God's name in previous experiences of Christianity. Radical inclusivity intentionally creates ministry on the margin, and its goal is *not* to imitate mainline expressions of church. It involves a new way of seeing and being that transcends our humanity in order "to see each other as God

---

229 Jersak, *A More Christlike Way*, p. 132.
230 Flunder, *Where the Edge Gathers*, pp. x-xi.
231 Ibid., p. xii.
232 Ibid., p. xiv.
233 Ibid., p. 25.
234 Ibid.
235 Ibid., pp. 134-137.
236 Ibid., p. 134.

sees us."[237] A sustainable radical inclusivity requires destigmatizing educa-tion (awareness, information, and understanding) with a relational ethic. It does not hide in shame or fear but seeks to "undo" both shame and fear, so that there is freedom to fully be "who their Creator has made them."[238] Radical inclusivity recognizes diversity within marginality; common life together on the margin does not imply affirmation of differences or that commonalities will hold them together. Hospitality acknowledges that ev-eryone already is welcomed by God; the welcoming invitation is to claim that seat at the table. Responsibility and accountability are the keys for sustainability in Flunder's model, requiring the effort of everyone in the community to live a celebratory life that is free and mutually contributory for the well-being for all.[239]

Providing safe and supportive space where marginalized people are free to be who they are, to use their own voices, and to vulnerably grow through living together with others in an accepting and dignifying cul-ture is a community where "individuals begin to 'see' themselves and each other through the eyes of faith…the eyes of God."[240] Often churches and neighborhoods are not heterogenous enough to practice this kind of com-mon life on the margins. Flunder boldly asserts that "there is an over-whelming need to *take the church to the edge rather than seeking to bring the margin to the center*" (emphasis mine).[241] Admittedly, this is something many mainstream Christians fear despite the model of Jesus living a life on the margins and the early church being defined by its marginality in society and religion from its onset. We must scatter to the margins to gather authentically in a common life of radical, inclusive love.

In *Abuelita Faith*, Kat Armas echoes Flunder's statement about decen-tralizing space; rather than making "space at the table for people on the margins" in an effort to bring the margin to the center, she insists, "People

---

237 Ibid., p. 136.
238 Ibid.
239 Ibid., pp. 134-137.
240 Ibid., p. 40.
241 Ibid., p. 131.

on the margins have their own tables."[242] Just as Jesus "turned table practices on their head" by, for example, "engaging and dignifying women of
questionable purity in table fellowship settings, which were male-domi-
nated and elite spaces," so should we do the same.[243] Rather than insisting on being hosts, kingdom hospitality requires the dominant culture to
decenter—to leave their own tables and the dominant narratives spoken
there to become "regular guests at unfamiliar tables with only the motives
of listening and learning."[244] Pohl relates that historically and presently,
the most transformative expressions of hospitality occur through hosts
on the margins that become bridges for social change.[245] The twenty-first
century embodiment of a common life must engage in a decolonized hospitality where conversations about real life struggles and raw grassroots
faith recenter the good news of Christ through the welcoming hosts of
tables on the margins of dominant culture.[246] A decolonized hospitality
embodies an iconic mosaic of the full image of God through each culture,
people, and group, pointing toward the future kingdom banqueting table
where all are welcomed by a Restorer who one day will restore all things,
righting all wrongs.

Within the framework of our human fragility, radical hospitality takes
risks. We are vulnerable people who struggle with our desire and capacity
for openness and our fear and distrust of the unfamiliar. We live amidst
restlessness and doubt and despair, chaos and betrayal. We long for connection and meaning in life. We desire to be seen and known with authenticity. We struggle with our ability to communicate clearly and our inability to correctly interpret the messages of others who see life differently; we
also experience the stranger's frustration to do the same. Moyaert states
that restraint is necessary for the unfolding of our different worlds to each
other. "The other who asks to be understood and comprehended challenges the interpreter to listen and to make room in his own identity for the

---

242 Kat Armas, *Abuelita Faith: What Women on the Margins Teach Us About Wisdom, Persistence, and Strength* (Grand Rapids, MI: BrazosPress, 2021), p. 137.
243 Ibid.; See also, Luke 7:37 for one example of this.
244 Ibid.
245 Pohl, *Making Room*, p. 106
246 Armas, *Abuelita Faith*, p. 137.

strange."[247] We sense these limitations and paradoxical tensions that affect our identities in our bodies, emotions, intellect, and spirits. "Fragility and vulnerability point to the idea that the ability and inability, choice and given, autonomy and heteronomy, capacity and incapacity continually go hand in hand in the human being."[248]

Subversively, a common life that embodies hospitality with strangers becomes a place of paradox where human experiences of joy and pain are woven together with hope that love is possible. "The gift of hope embedded in these communities of hospitality nourishes, challenges, and transforms guests, hosts, and sometimes the larger community."[249] People are both shaped by and invited into a hospitable common life.[250] From a spiritual standpoint, God enters through the hospitable door and outpours himself into the common life, making room for love "where two or three gather together."[251] The Spirit of God inhabits such places. Knowing that not everything is possible for small and fragile humans, God does not reject nor condemn human fragility, vulnerability, or restlessness as people are confronted with and struggle through their suffering including, "the violence of nature, with injustice, with love and being in love, passion, and rage."[252] Lovingly, God enters the common life to bring peace and rest through a feast, making room for all to commune together.

A feast puts a halt to the everyday toil. Feasts turn us away from scarcity to enjoy generosity and abundance, "creating a distance to the everyday understood as cares, work, struggle."[253] Feasts break through space and time and the struggles and silences between us to create openness and celebration through food and drink, music and dancing. We feast in spite of the hardships in life and the celebration is a prophetic dissent, affirming that there is a transcendent reality beyond our everyday struggles.[254] "Cel-

---

247 Moyaert, *Fragile Identities*, p. 266.
248 Ibid., p. 281.
249 Pohl, *Making Room*, pp. 10–11.
250 Wirzba, *Food and Faith*, p. 50.
251 Matthew 18:20.
252 Moyaert, *Fragile Identities*, p. 290.
253 Ibid., pp. 301–302.
254 Ibid., pp. 301–305.

ebrating together creates solidarity and community. Eating and drinking together loosens the tongue and everyone *can* speak with everyone."[255] Feasting opens us up to our senses beyond the struggle to dialogue with each other; we experience our otherness through tasting and touching, through hearing and seeing and smelling. By suspending everyday life, the feast transcends human impotence and transforms the relationships within it.[256] As a result, the feast begins to overturn the underpinnings of how we treat each other every day. As the Spirit of Jesus hovers amidst the festal gathering, a resurrection of faith, hope, and love remains, pointing to a future reconciliation, a restoration of all that was lost in earthly reality.

The theme of hospitality, and in particular the idea of feasts, was central in the spiritual practice of "breaking of bread" together in the common life of the Jesus Way in the book of Acts. In remembrance of Israel's liberation story, Jesus revealed himself as the broken bread and poured out wine in his Last Supper with his disciples. Luu explains that "Jesus reinterprets the Passover, portraying it as a story of deliverance rather than one of vengeance. Similarly, the cup and bread point to the self-sacrifice of Jesus and not toward the "sacrifice for" aspect of the Passover meal. Jesus is not saying that God needs a sacrifice in order to free us; he is saying that God does free us, and this freedom involves a self-giving God."[257]

Christ's presence is "not just as host; he is also the feast."[258] Christ is also the guest and the "slave" serving the table![259] This idea that Jesus himself is the Feast—giving himself as food for the life of the world—was retained as a meal in the ordinary domestic setting of the home for over two hundred years for the early church.[260] Every time the early church gathered, in some cases daily, they were nourished by bread and wine in remembrance of Christ's "ongoing presence and activity in the Church—

---

255 Ibid., 305
256 Ibid. pp. 304-306.
257 Phuc Luu, *Jesus of the East*, p. 138.
258 Richard M. Spielmann, *The History of Christian Worship* (New York: The Seabury Press, 1966), p. 17.; See also John 6:51-56.
259 I am grateful to Chris Green for these insights.
260 Ibid., p. 19.

past, present, and future."[261] This created a "holistic approach to spirituality that celebrated God's holy presence in, with, and among them as they came together."[262]

To partake in Jesus as the Feast, through ordinary bread and wine "is to join in a *re-membering* of a world *dis-membered* by sin."[263] Breaking bread in remembrance of Jesus as the Feast, central to the common life of Jesus followers, witnesses to Christ's ongoing presence in the world—a restorative "putting back together again" as a dis-membered world is re-membered through self-giving love. Jesus reveals himself in the "breaking of the bread," and then nourishes, strengthens, sustains, transforms and inspires the guests around an inclusive table.[264] We are inspired to remember the "least of these." The breaking of bread demonstrates that we can no longer relate to people transactionally or in utilitarian ways, but with a welcoming love expressed through attention, forgiveness, healing, and reconciliation.[265]

The "breaking of bread" is an icon of the future kingdom of love. Schmemann enlightens, "Through love God created the world...Through love he sent his only begotten Son...And now, at this table, he manifests and grants this love as his kingdom, and his kingdom as 'abiding' in love."[266] As we eat and drink, we celebrate God's good creation and his generous, universal love for all of God's creatures. We truly participate in a love feast. The feast is a foretaste "here and now of what will come at the eschaton."[267] In solidarity with marginalized people the feast is eaten with faith for truth and reconciliation. The breaking of bread shared in a common life built with neighbors and strangers unveils the possibilities that living an inclusive life with people in the margins means that the Spirit can break through societal structures in the same ways that Jesus did

261 Winfield Bevins, *Ever Ancient, Ever New: The Allure of Liturgy for a New Generation* (Grand Rapids, MI: Zondervan, 2019), p. 61.
262 Ibid., p. 62.
263 Wirzba, *Faith and Food*, p. 201.
264 Ibid., pp. 200-201.
265 Ibid., p. 209.
266 Alexander Schmemann, *The Eucharist: Sacrament of the Kingdom* (Crestwood, NY: St. Vladimir's Seminary Press, 2003), pp. 200-201.
267 Moyaert, *Fragile Identities*, p. 310.

around the tables of his day.[268] God's table *must* be open since *all* hungry people are welcomed into this inclusive community of love.[269] At God's feast, each and every one of us must be taken, blessed, broken, and given for the healing and reconciliation of the world.[270] Moyaert explains,

> ...we must give because life is given to us. In the feast the fullness of life is celebrated. God loves to be loved, thus let us love one another in the feast. Does this remove the conflict? No. Does this make the fragility of human life disappear? No here as well. But the sense that God has done more for human beings (logic of abundance) than they deserve also offers them the power to do more than they must (logic of equivalence), and in that way people already work here and now for the hoped for reconciliation.[271]

Heath relates that we can never celebrate God's love too much since we see in the life of Jesus the God who thoroughly lives into the "messy, troubled, and ordinary neighborhoods of this world."[272]

Although this type of hospitable space seems idealistic, optimistic, and even difficult to implement in institutional church settings, it is not inconceivable to imagine from the perspective of the "kitchen theology" of "abuelita faith." Armas explains that abuelita theology recognizes the wisdom of unnamed grandmothers as the embodiment of everyday faith, love, and hope. They were not merely teachers of prescribed doctrinal truths, but they nurtured the Spirit's sense of making all things new in everyday life.[273] "Some call abuelita theology 'kitchen theology' because it is formed in the kitchen—while frijoles negros (black beans) are sim-

---

268 Ibid., p. 311.
269 Lapish, "The Lord's Supper Table," pp. 133-143.
270 Elaine A. Heath, *The Healing Practice of Celebration* (Nashville, TN: Abingdon Press, 2020), p. 47.
271 Moyaert, *Fragile Identities*, p. 313.
272 Ibid., p. 44.
273 Armas, *Abuelita Faith*, p. 33.

mering on the stove, the floor is being mopped, and the cafecito (coffee) is brewing. Abuelita theology takes form while family members are sitting around the mesa (the table) discussing la lucha, the struggle of everyday life."[274] The struggles of life and matters of faith are embodied, reflected upon, and wrestled with, and over time, theology and spirituality emerges, evolves, and transforms the conversation partners in ordinary, informal spaces. "The work of theology is a work of the people, something we do en conjunto, together. In this way, the image of God is not just individual but collective."[275]

Perhaps a reorientation of *sacred space* is called for to decolonize perceptions of the church in the ancient-future spiritual practice of the common life and the breaking of bread in our day. Counterintuitively, perhaps expressions of church must grow smaller to expand our capacity for inclusivity, for being human together, so that neighbors are loved in the midst of our mutual human fragility, vulnerability, and fallibility. Ordinary hospitality within homes can foster diverse friendships in a welcoming space of safety and rest, for storytelling and testimony, for wrestling together and working together, for facing each other and feasting with each other. Perhaps, with the recovery of an inclusive love feast around the real tables of Jesus followers, the diverse family of God would grow in love and in understanding together, organically and peacefully bearing kingdom fruit to transform our communities. Just as "the Word became flesh and blood and moved into the neighborhood,"[276] hospitable openness in our homes, inclusive and in the margins, can become the locus for the embodiment of Jesus as we share his good news stories.

274 Ibid., p. 20.
275 Ibid., p. 28.
276 John 1:14, *The Message*

Ancient-Future Spiritual Practices of Being and Acting: Apostolic Instruction and Prayer

The stories of scripture are "messy and multilayered," full of complex and contradictory human experience.[277] Armas suggests that in the recognition of seeing the complexity of human stories within scripture narratives, our ways of seeing and engaging each other can shift.[278] "We tell these stories because they are stories of God existing in the gray with God's people, of God journeying alongside them in the messiness of what it means to be human, of what it means to survive—and even attempt to thrive—in the midst of oppressive empires, in exile, in between two worlds."[279]

Puhalo states that the overarching unifying story found in the pages of scripture "is about us, and it is also about God's infinite love and mercy."[280] Scripture becomes a "mirror into which we gaze and see the reflection of our own selves" through Spirit-infused stories revealing God's love and mercy—the unveiled gospel in the "face of Christ."[281] Enns states that the Bible does not call attention to itself, but affirms Puhalo's mirror imagery; the Bible says, "look *through* me."[282] The Bible decenters itself, Enns says, to reveal Jesus as the center. "All of the holy scriptures point to him—Israel's scriptures point forward to him, the New Testament points back to him, the gospels portray him."[283] A christotelic hermeneutic, sees scripture as a whole finding its consummation (*telos*) in Christ with a trajectory that continues in the beloved community today.[284]

A christotelic interpretation of scripture discloses a gospel-focused message fulfilled in Jesus that truly is good news for all people because

---

277 Armas, *Abuelita Faith*, p. 172.
278 Ibid.
279 Ibid.
280 Lazar Puhalo, *The Mirror of Scripture: The Old Testament Is About You* (Abbotsford, BC: St. Macrina Press, 2018), p. 13.
281 Ibid., p. 208; 2 Corinthians 4:1-6.
282 Peter Enns, *The Bible Tells Me So: Why Defending Scripture Has Made Us Unable To Read It* (New York: HarperOne, 2014), p. 237.
283 Jason Byassee, *Surprised by Jesus Again: Reading the Bible in Communion With the Saints* (Grand Rapids, MI: William B. Eerdmans Publishing Company, 2019), p. 139.
284 Enns, "Apostolic Hermeneutics," p. 277; see also Brad Jersak, *A More Christlike Word*, p. 17-20.

God is Liberator and humankind is "one family united under the rule of Christ whose death for sins reconciles us to God."[285] Jesus' self-proclaimed and embodied fulfillment of Isaiah 61:1-2a found in Luke 4: 17-21 is the liberation theology that is good news to the poor, freedom for prisoners of every bondage, recovery of sight for the blinded, and liberating release for the oppressed—in a word: Jubilee.[286] In *Reading While Black*, McCaulley contends that "the cross functions as the *end of the cycle of vengeance and death* and that the cross is a place where God enters into our pain."[287] Reading *through* scripture we encounter Jesus as the Way together as a liberating "journey of growing and stretching and questioning."[288]

Through scripture, states professor of public theology at Southeastern University, Chris E.W. Green, humans struggle with God and with each other, with questions and with discoveries, ancient and new. Amidst God's texts, the infinite Spirit illuminates endless possibilities for interpretation that have potential for transforming us together in good and beautiful ways to enact the works of God faithfully and presently in our world as peacemakers.[289] Green elaborates on Origen's commentary from the *Philocalia* 6.1-2, that the way of blessing for peacemakers is demonstrated by the way they handle the scriptures. Green explains,

> First, peacemakers discover the peace *of* the Scriptures, which are at peace in the sense that they manifest one unified witness to Jesus Christ. Second, peacemakers know how to make peace *with* the Scriptures, reconciling the seeming contradictions within the texts—and the real contradictions between themselves and the texts—as well

285 Esau McCaulley, *Reading While Black: African-American Biblical Interpretation as an Exercise in Hope* (Downers Grove, IL: IVP Academic, 2020), p. 19.
286 Wright, *Acts for Everyone*, p.75.
287 Ibid., p. 122.; Jacqueline Grant, *White Women's Christ and Black Women's Jesus: Feminist Christology and Womanist Response* (Atlanta, GA: Scholars Press, 1989), p. 221.Womanist theology attests to the tri-dimensional embodiment of racism, sexism, and classism in the experience of Black women as a testimony that a constructive, wholistic Christology must be a liberating one.
288 Flood, *Disarming Scripture*, p. 257.
289 Green, *Sanctifying Interpretation*, preface to 2nd edition, pp. xi – xv.

as discerning the deeper, hidden significances of seemingly meaningless passages. That is why, peacemaking interpreters find that they are also making peace with and for their neighbors, discovering and helping others discover the peace of God.[290]

Hall asserts that the ancient scriptural hermeneutic demonstrated through "the church fathers on Scripture possesses the flexibility and responsiveness to meet the interpretive and ethical challenges the contemporary world poses."[291] Gleaning wisdom from the ancient fathers' interpretive lens necessitates a listening posture, humility, and a self-awareness that silences our past prejudices.[292] Their approach is worthy of examination and emulation.

One of the most crucial patristic insights is the connection they make between the interpretive reading of scripture and the interpreter's spiritual character formation. Spiritual formation through the scriptures was a call to both "wholeness and integrity, to allow our lives to be shaped by the narrative of Scripture" within the faith community.[293] Scriptural exegesis was evident as it was embodied. As the interpreter was spiritually formed by scripture, those texts were actively displayed in daily life. Spiritual formation through obedience was a "listening that leads to action."[294] As people wrestle *through* scripture seeking to obey Jesus' new commandment, they are transformed *by* the love of God *for* love of neighbor *as* we love ourselves. In so doing, people enflesh what Augustine described as a hermeneutic of love. "Whoever, then, thinks that he understands the Holy Scriptures, or any part of them, but puts such an interpretation

---

290 Ibid., pp. xii-xiii.
291 Christopher A. Hall, *Reading Scripture with the Church Fathers* (Downers Grove, IL: InterVarsity Press, 1998), p. 31.
292 Ibid., p. 36.
293 Ibid., pp. 41-42.
294 Heath, *The Healing Practice*, p. 52.

upon them as does not tend to build up this twofold love of God and our neighbor, does not yet understand them as he ought."[295]

Recovering a patristic hermeneutic elucidates a contemporary model for apostolic instruction in the gatherings of the Jesus Way that promotes a return to reading scripture with Christ as the Word made flesh. Jesus—his incarnation, life, death, burial, resurrection, and his reign—is the fulfillment of the Law and Prophets and Psalms as revealed through the writings of scripture.[296] According to Green, a patristic interpretive reading makes present the works of God as readers discover the spirit of scripture beyond the letters of the words on the page; it is a Pentecostal, Spirit-led way of reading.[297] Gleaning from the way Jesus revealed the scriptures concerning himself in Luke 24: 13-27, Jersak refers to the *Emmaus Way* as the key for understanding how the early apostles and church fathers read scripture and embodied it with love for God and love for neighbor.[298] This approach is an example of what Green calls a reading that is "good," not merely on the basis of its careful exegesis of what the text meant for its first listeners, but because of the interpretation's beautiful effects to "bring the peace of God to bear on the world."[299] Patristic interpretation has potential for revitalizing apostolic instruction for the Jesus Way that can become a Spirit-led and embodied witness of peace in the world today.

In *A More Christlike Word: Reading Scripture the Emmaus Way,* Bradley Jersak, Dean of Theology and Culture at St. Stephen's University, gives the essence of patristic interpretation for restoring an apostolic way of reading scripture. Unlike the literalism of contemporary biblicists, the early church used a "literal sense" as a *first* layer of reading to honor the words of scripture within its historical framework and within its literary genres. The literal sense of the early church fathers involved textual criticism, genre analysis, and lexical exegesis which continues today with the

---

295 Augustine, *On Christian Doctrine,* 1.36.40; available online: www.ntslibrary.com/PDF%20Books/Augustine%20doctrine.pdf; accessed February 16, 2022.
296 Luke 24: 44; Matthew 5:17-18.
297 Green, *Sanctifying Interpretation,* p. xiv.
298 Jersak, *A More Christlike Word: Reading Scripture the Emmaus Way* (New Kensington, PA: Whitaker House, 2021), pp. 127-138; see also Luke 24: 13-27.
299 Green, *Sanctifying Interpretation,* p. xiii.

work of textual analysis, translation, and commentary among contemporary scholars. Through careful exegesis and following "the rules of sound interpretation" listed above, the literal sense of meaning was discovered in the words of scripture.[300]

Based on the foundational *literal* sense of scripture, the other layers of an apostolic reading revealed the *spiritual* sense of the scripture—the allegorical, moral, and anagogical meanings disclosed as the Holy Spirit interpreted sacred texts through the worshipping and discerning community.[301] The *allegorical* sense of scripture illuminates through typology and allegory that "a biblical text possesses a deeper meaning in light of God's action in Christ."[302] This spiritual sense of the text demonstrates that the Law and the Prophets consistently pointed to Christ's incarnation, life, death, resurrection, and his reign, and therefore, the whole story of scripture is a fluid movement toward revealing Christ as its *telos*, its completion or fulfillment. The allegorical interpretation asks, *"How might any given Old Testament text point to Christ and his gospel?"*[303]

Jersak points out that this is not a "non-Jewish" interpretation, but rather, demonstrates the manner in which a *particular* Jewish rabbi, Jesus Christ, interpreted those Jewish sacred writings; his disciples use Christ's interpretive method.[304] Jesus demonstrates this spiritual method in his Sermon on the Mount interpretation of the Law in his "You have heard it said….but I say to you" statements in Matthew 5:17-48 as well as his

---

300 Jersak, *A More Christlike Word*, pp. 129-131; See Christopher A. Hall, *Reading Scripture*, p. 132 where Hall relates the points of agreement of the eight doctors of the Church in the East (Athanasius, Gregory of Nazianzus, Basil the Great, and John Chrysostom) and the West (Ambrose, Jerome, Augustine, and Gregory the Great): "All agreed that the Bible is an inspired text. All agreed that personal disposition and spiritual health affect one's ability to read Scripture well. All agreed that once the exegete has determined the meaning of a biblical text and plumbed its possible applications, the text's inherent divine authority summons the biblical interpreter to obedience. All agreed that biblical interpretation is a Christian communal endeavor, and the exegete must practice within the context of Christ's body, the church. Most possessed a profound respect for the exegetical efforts of other interpreters in the church's history, even when they disagreed with their conclusions. Exegesis is never, the fathers argued, to be practiced in a historical, traditional or communal vacuum."

301 Jersak, *A More Christlike Word*, pp. 121-131.

302 Christopher A. Hall, *Reading Scripture*, p. 134.

303 Jersak, *A More Christlike Word*, p. 135.

304 Ibid., pp. 140-141.

interpretation of the story of Jonah as a "sign" referring to his death, burial and resurrection in Matthew 12:38-41. He does the same on the Emmaus Road in Luke 24: 13-35 as he shows himself to be the fulfillment of the words of Moses and the prophecies of suffering found in Isaiah and elsewhere. According to Hall,[305] Jesus modeled an allegorical interpretation of scripture that the apostle Paul continued as he unveiled Hebrew scriptures in I Corinthians 10:1-6 through the typology of Israel in Egypt and in the wilderness and in Galatians 4:24-26 as allegories of Hagar and Sarah reflecting deeper Christian realities. Instruction through many of the Apostolic Fathers continued this interpretive tradition.[306] In essence, the *allegorical* sense of scripture ultimately points to Jesus himself as the Word of God. "Thus, to read Scripture in its spiritual sense is, in fact, to read it as the cruciform gospel."[307]

The second spiritual sense of interpreting scripture is the *moral* sense. According to Jersak,

> The moral reading of the text asks this question of any given Scripture: *"How will this passage nourish my growth as a follower of Jesus Christ?"* That is, *"How will it transform me so that the truth of my being (the image of Christ) becomes the way of my being (the likeness of Christ)?"* The *moral* meaning, then, is also *tropological* (it transforms the will) and *existential* (it addresses my real-life dilemmas).[308]

In other words, the *moral* sense of reading scripture is apostolic instruction for both personal transformation through God's love and for enacting that love with justice and mercy in the world.

The last layer of spiritual reading in the apostolic instruction of the early church was *anagogical* sense, leading to "view realities and events in

---

305 Hall, *Reading Scripture*, pp. 133-134.
306 Ibid., pp. 132-155.
307 Jersak, *A More Christlike Word*, p. 134.
308 Ibid., p. 132.

70

terms of their eternal significance, leading us toward our true homeland: thus the Church on earth is a sign of the heavenly Jerusalem."[309] This speaks to the kingdom of God eschaton, where all will finally be restored. It encourages continued labors to bring the gospel to bear on the earth in the here and now while awaiting with faith, hope, and love, and reminding followers of the ultimate restoration to come.

Hall illuminates that patristic insights for interpreting scripture for apostolic instruction came through "knowledge conceived in the womb of prayer and worship."[310] Scripture meditation was grounded in prayer through the illumination of the Holy Spirit. In the classic spiritual memoir, *Confessions*, Augustine, confesses his despair with interpreting scripture from merely a literal sense and was impressed as he observed how Ambrose read scripture meditatively. Ambrose humbly modeled a deeply reverent and contemplative reading of sacred script for the spiritual sense of layered meanings in the text.[311] Augustine embraced Ambrose's contemplative posture with scripture as is evident in his prayerful cries for discernment as he wrestled with scripture and sought to be transformed by the spirit of those texts as he journaled in his *Confessions*.[312] The experiential and meditative approach toward reading scripture for its spiritual sense (allegorical, moral, and anagogical) that Ambrose and Augustine modeled in the fourth century Western Church foreshadowed the sacred reading, or *lectio divina,* that Benedict of Nursia would later develop in the fifth century. *Lectio divina* would characterize how scripture reading was approached for the first 1500 years of church history.[313]

Calhoun describes the movements of *lectio divina* as: *silencio, lectio, meditatio, oratio,* and *contemplatio.*[314] This type of scripture reading is not primarily concerned with the literal study or interpretation of textual in-

309 Ibid., p. 131.
310 Hall, *Reading Scripture*, p. 151.
311 Augustine, *The Confessions*, trans. Maria Boulding (New York: Vintage Books, 1998), pp. 94-99.
312 Ibid., pp. 175-178; 201; 241-242; 325.
313 Adele Ahlberg Calhoun, *Spiritual Disciplines Handbook: Practices That Transform Us* (Downers Grove, IL: IVP Books, 2015), p. 188; See also Ruth Haley Barton, *Sacred Rhythms: Arranging Our Lives for Spiritual Transformation* (Downers Grove, IL: IVP Books, 2006), p. 54.
314 Calhoun, *Spiritual Disciplines Handbook*, pp. 188-189.

formation as much as the spiritual transformation of the reader. "Refer-ring to the material being read and the method itself, the practice of *lectio divina* is rooted in the belief that through the presence of the Holy Spirit, the Scriptures are indeed alive and active as we engage them for spiritual transformation."[315] *Silencio* commences the practice of *lectio divina* as the heart is prepared quietly and receptively for God's presence. In the process of *lectio divina,* a short passage of scripture is read aloud slowly 4 consecu-tive times, followed by a reflective question and a period of silence. In the first movement, or *lectio,* the scripture passage is read aloud as the listener (or reader) notices and attends to a word or phrase that resonates within the heart. In *meditatio,* as the passage is read a second time, the word or phrase is reflected upon more deeply as the listener asks questions with curiosity about the highlighted phrase in the text. The third movement, *oratio,* is the heart's responsive prayer to the challenges or invitations pre-sented through attentive listening as the scripture is read a third time. The final reading becomes *contemplatio,* a restful communion with God en-abling the faithful response of living out the word (*incarnatio)* as a prayer-ful embodied response to meditation on scripture throughout the day.[316] To summarize, spiritual director and contemplative teacher, Lisa Colon Delay, states that the process of *lectio divina* involves reading, reflecting, responding, and resting in God's presence.[317] Through the process of *lectio divina,* the spiritual sense of scripture (allegorical, moral, and anagogical) can be discovered and discerned for personal transformation that leads to an embodied response.

A regular practice of *lectio divina* and contemplative prayer posture might also lead to more skillfully discerning the spirit of the voices pres-ent while reading scripture. Jersak states that "the whole Bible is true as it tells *one* ongoing story of the people of God through this polyphony of voices."[318] The one ongoing faith story, however, is told by contrast-ing two revelations. The first revelation is "sacrificial religion" defined as

315 Barton, *Sacred Rhythms,* p. 309.
316 Barton, *Sacred Rhythms,* pp. 48-61; Calhoun, *Spiritual Disciplines Handbook,* pp. 188-191.
317 Delay, *The Wild Land Within: Cultivating Wholeness Through Spiritual Practice* (Minneapolis: Broadleaf Books, 2021), p. 143.
318 Jersak, *A More Christlike Word,* p. 201.

the "fallen state of humanity and its broken images of God" wherein we hear the retributive cacophony of voices of the accuser, the victim, and the law. These voices call for punishment, vengeance, and sacrifice. The second revelation is the restorative voice of "self-giving love" defined as "humanity restored in Jesus who incarnates the true image of God." This singular voice, Jersak calls "the voice of the Lamb" who speaks words and actions of mercy, forgiveness, and reconciliation. Although all of these voices belong and are part of the story, the voices must be spiritually discerned.[319] Death-dealing voices of sacrificial religion come to "steal, kill and destroy."[320] Life-giving voices of self-giving love come to bring life restoratively and abundantly. A reflective reading of scripture makes room for the wise discernment of spiritual voices within the text.

In addition to the meditative way of reading scripture anchored in the ancient Western Church tradition, contemplative prayer practices stemming from the ancient Eastern Church are making a resurgence in recent years. Delay distinguishes between the Western and Eastern conceptions of spiritual formation. Spiritual formation in the West tends toward "the more cerebral and academic, while Eastern concepts tend to be more incarnational and embodied."[321] Delay describes spiritual formation in the East within a paradigm of wholeness. "In the East, the inherent goodness of all God created and the human dependence on God are at the core of theological understanding."[322] Central to the idea of sin is "human fallibility and vulnerability, not ancestral debts," so the emphasis of spiritual growth is on continual healing what is sick in us through ongoing *theosis*—being made into the likeness of God toward full restoration and union with God.[323]

---

319 Ibid., pp. 201-213.
320 John 10: 1-18.
321 Delay, *The Wild Land Within*, p. 27.
322 Ibid., p. 31.
323 Ibid.; See also Phuc Luu, *Jesus of the East*, p. 139 further describing the idea of *theosis*. He states, "Jesus' work in the world was to restore the *imago Dei* in each of us so that we might live in ways that bring life and meaning throughout the world. The purpose of restoration is to make us like God (not God, but *like* God), a process that the Eastern fathers called *theosis.*"

Wholeness as *beings* connects the body, emotions, and intellect with spirituality, and therefore, spiritual practices that encompass all aspects of selfhood bring spiritual growth and healing to the "wild land within."[324] Contemplative prayer practices begin with *hesychasm,* an orienting posture of stillness, solitude, and silence. This allows for a watchful attentiveness to God's presence, or *nepsis,* in which a deepened awareness to egoistic emotions, motivations, and thoughts are brought to awareness. With awareness, these selfish thoughts are released as attentive focus is given to God's presence. The emphasis is on *being* with God, without words, rather than *doing* or communicating through words; it is an intimate prayer of communion with God.

Contemplative prayer practices include breath prayer, centering prayer, and the Jesus prayer in various forms, and they can promote healing in our bodies, emotions, minds, and spirits, according to Delay.[325] Another traditional form of contemplative prayer, the examen developed in the fifteenth century by St. Ignatius of Loyola, is helpful for practicing the presence of God throughout the activities of life. A periodic reflection throughout the day to give thanks, to notice life-giving moments, and to recognize when love and connection with God was experienced, helps to promote mindfulness. A recognition of instances and patterns where connection with God and others was lost, or experiences that were not life-giving, or love was not given, also facilitates daily discernment of spiritual, mental, emotional, and physical wellbeing.[326]

Contemporary research also demonstrates that contemplative prayer practices facilitate collective trauma healing in times of crisis. Delay asserts that contemplative spirituality among marginalized groups demonstrates the ways spiritual formation is forged through oppression, collective trauma, and suffering to reframe the gospel for community healing. The climate of interior landscapes affects spiritual formation and margin-

---

324 Ibid., pp. 33-34. Delay emphasizes the significant influence of ethnicity, race, gender, biology, and economic status on personal spirituality and highlights specific contemplative practices and rituals found in Native American, Latinx, Asian, and African spiritualities in the Americas in Chapter 3 entitled "Climate as Context: Centering Marginalized Voices," pp. 37-60.

325 Ibid., pp. 111-122.

326 Calhoun, *Spiritual Disciplines Handbook,* pp. 59-60.

alized voices must be centered for truth, reconciliation, and healing—for finding a home in the divine love within self and extended to the wider community.[327] In this space, the Holy Spirit is actively moving to help people transcend hatred and bring hope in times of crisis through "communal resilience and peaceful resistance."[328]

The rediscovery of the ancient *lectio divina* approach for reading scripture from the West, as well as a more widespread use of ancient contemplative prayer practices from the East, would result in a wholistic spiritual formation, both personally and communally. These approaches require a robust pneumatology in belief and practice in order to trust the Holy Spirit's transformative power to teach, guide, reveal, convict, and transform *through* scripture and reflective prayer. The apostolic instruction of the early church with its multi-layered christotelic interpretive approach (literal, allegorical, moral, anagogical) guards against a purely literal rendering of sacred texts, most notably the toxic texts of terror, especially when the polyphony of voices are spiritually discerned, and textual fulfillment is centered on the good news of Christ. Safe and diverse hospitable spaces of radical inclusion on the margins can make room for stories to be voiced with freedom and handled with care (and with feasting) as our humanity is mirrored through scripture and through the stories of a God who is love. Collective trauma healing could be a hopeful outcome of gatherings of the Jesus Way that scatters incarnationally to love neighbors and to build peace in times of community crisis.

How might spiritual formation in the Western Church be reoriented through ancient contemplative prayer practices and an apostolic hermeneutic for scripture reading around an inclusive hospitable table with diverse neighbors to revitalize the fourfold "ways of the Jesus Way" today? Would the accessible grassroots discovery approach of the Global South and East mesh with the spiritual practices of the ancient church to fulfill

---

327 Delay, *The Wild Land Within*, pp. 145-179.; See also Barbara A. Holmes, *Crisis Contemplation: Healing the Wounded Village* (Albuquerque, NM: CAC Publishing, 2021), pp. 11-59. Holmes explores "crisis contemplation as a gift of liminality and an opportunity for bio-spiritual resurrection," p. 13.
328 Holmes, *Crisis Contemplation*, p. 134.

the predictions of scholarly interlocutors for theological education so that the future Church flourishes as an authentic witness to the self-giving love of Jesus Christ? A contemporary remix of the fourfold ancient spiritual practices with a discovery approach for belonging, being, and acting together as the beloved community will be proposed for the Jesus Way forward.

CHAPTER 6

A NEIGHBORLY WAY FORWARD

A Contemplative Discovery Approach

In her bold and prophetic little book entitled, *God Unbound: Wisdom from Galatians for the Anxious Church,* Elaine Heath urges Jesus followers to get out of the four walls of the church and into their neighborhoods to enflesh the Sermon on the Mount with "spiritually deep yet nimble expressions of church."[329] She imagines a global, Spirit-led, grassroots "gospel-shaped movement of Jesus" which is "one that finds solidarity with 'the least of these' and is accessible to and largely led by laypeople."[330] Heath envisions a living *into* the radical inclusivity of Galatians 3:27-29 where new expressions of church more fully embody the multicultural and egalitarian Jesus Way of the early church where *all* are one in Christ, *all* can be filled with the Holy Spirit, and *all* can minister through the gifts given by the Spirit.

As the social structures and systems in our culture and faith communities flatten, new forms of gathering "defy containment in a church building" to celebrate diversity of all kinds—beyond the spectrum of binaries which divide humanity—beyond political, denominational, racial, ethnic, gender, religious, and social class categories.[331] Besides being diverse, these new expressions, "tend to be smaller, less ambitious, [and] more fluid,"; they are humble and hospitable and have a kingdom of God

---

329 Elaine Heath, *God Unbound: Wisdom From Galatians for the Anxious Church* (Nashville, TN: Upper Room Books, 2016), pp. 9-10.
330 Ibid., p. 10.
331 Ibid., pp. 10-11.

orientation.[332] They work to "discover God's activity in the neighborhood and to join in."[333] Heath continues,

> While they believe that they are bringing Jesus *to* the neighborhood, they are also meeting Jesus *in* the neighborhood. This posture differs from the insider/outsider mindset that is common in the inherited church. And while they welcome people into the gatherings, they do not believe that the goal of loving neighbor is to colonize them culturally. They take seriously the simple words of Jesus about God loving both the just and the unjust. They choose to give up all forms of control, manipulation, and colonization in the name of evangelism and mission.[334]

Heath suggests that since the Church has lost its privileged voice in society, we should remember our spiritual heritage and origin story. The Jesus Way has always done its best work on the bottom or the edge or from the margins of society.[335] She calls forth creativity, discovery, and "failing our way forward" as we experiment with approaches and styles of communal Christian spiritual formation that express the Way in the future for the flourishing of our neighborhoods.[336]

One such experimental approach builds on the research presented throughout this book. The Discovery Bible Study (DBS) method was initially developed in the margins of organically emerging Disciple Making Movements in the Global South. I propose a contemplative reframing of

---

332 Ibid., pp. 56-59.
333 Ibid., p. 58.
334 Ibid.
335 Ibid., p. 98.
336 Ibid., pp. 58; 100; Jordan, *Transforming Fire,* p. 155. Jordan agrees that now is the time for a wide range of experiments, insisting that "We need as many experiments with structures for sheltering theology as we can manage—with or without the blessing of accreditation and (forgive me) denominational approval...If the future of theological education in the United States looks to be poorer and smaller than what it has been, we might relearn from poor and small communities the power of the Word."

this model with an ancient-future reorientation for spiritual formation. It incorporates a christotelic, patristic hermeneutic for communal scripture reading in the context of radically inclusive hospitality with local neighbors. The Contemplative Discovery Approach (CDA) that I developed should not be considered a "method" as such; most of what I present is in the form of contemplative questions for consideration and vignettes that illustrate the *movement* of the approach. By encouraging faithful questioning, and by providing the present experimental approach as a way of belonging, being, and acting together in local neighborhoods, I hope to inspire imagination for other creative embodied expressions of Christ-like, Spirit-led, contemplative communities of spiritual practice in grass-roots local contexts.

Belonging: A Contemplative Discovery Approach for Hospitality in the Hood[337]

A group of local pastors and faith leaders met in a community building to discuss a model for uniting area churches for the purpose of saturating the community with gospel-centered love for their neighbors. One courageous pastor stood up and asked the conference leader a question that seemed to be in the heart of every pastor present. "How do we get our congregations to get involved with their neighbors—to meet them, to love them, and to serve them?" The conference speaker returned the question back to the group of pastors, "I don't know. That's for you to figure out. What do you think?" The silence was deafening, as the room filled with a communal poverty of spirit, a sense of repentant unknowing.[338]

---

337 Jennings, *After Whiteness*, p. 10. Jennings centralizes the necessity for cultivating a formational sense of belonging.

338 The italicized stories are based on true ones, told from my own memory and perspective as a participant or a facilitator in these experiences. I identify with Sara Miles' author's note, "To the best of my ability, I've tried to reconstruct events, chronology, and dialogue accurately, but there are inevitable errors and omissions. To use a religious analogy: The book is not the Bible imagined as inerrant and historically definitive. It's more the Bible I believe in—that is, a human compilation of stories told in different voices, edited and rearranged over many drafts to suggest truths not always

The institutional church has suffered deep loss and division in the past decades, now expedited even more deeply through global pandemic, racial and ethnic strife, and political divides.[339] Heath suggests that the institutional church is undergoing a "corporate dark night of the soul."[340] She explains that in the dark night, a "liberating love grows slowly and gradually."[341] Amidst great loss in the dark night emerges a deep longing for God.[342] "For the love of God is present and active in the night, bringing about growth, healing, and freedom" in hidden places.[343] Perhaps the mustard seed of love for God and love for neighbor is growing outside of our church buildings, planted in the hidden organic humus of neighborhood soil. Perhaps God actually *has* "moved into the neighborhood," as Peterson paraphrases in the *Message* Bible.[344]

Like the "expert in the law" in Luke 10:25-37, people in our neighborhoods have questions about the meaning of life and they have thoughtful and creative answers. And so do we. As Jesus followers we might know that the bottom-line spiritual response to life's questions is embedded in our foundational ethic: "Love the Lord your God with all your heart and

fully understood." Sara Miles, *Take This Bread: The Spiritual Memoir of a Twenty-First-Century Christian* (New York: Ballantine Books, 2007), p. x.

339 Smith, *Theological Education Between the Times,* inside book cover description. The entire premise in the *Theological Education Between the Times* book series affirms that the present cultural moment is "a time of deep change" for theological institutions that are the training ground for institutional church pastors and faith leaders of the future, and therefore, "diverse groups of people for critical, theological conversations about meanings and purposes of theological education" are needed for a reimagined vision.

340 Heath, *The Mystic Way,* p. 10.; Heath also cites pre-pandemic Barna research to show the steady decline in church memberships, an increasing percentage of Americans not attending church, fewer young adults preparing for ordained ministry, and the loss of moral credibility among faith leaders and in the churches among the possible signs of the "dark night," pp. 16-17.; Aleshire, *Beyond Profession,* p. 77. Aleshire concurs with these trends: "But the data over time do paint a picture of a declining positive view of the ethics of clergy (a drop of more than 20 percentage points in the past fifteen years) and declining confidence in organized religion (a drop of almost 30 percentage points from 1975-2018)."

341 Ibid., p. 21.

342 Ibid., p. 25.

343 Ibid., p. 20.

344 John 1:14, *Message*; Conde-Frazier, *Atando Cabos,* p. 117. Conde-Frazier suggests more informal and mobile spaces for theological reflection and that theologians reside within local communities.; Day, *Notes of a Native Daughter,* pp. 126-129. Day foresees theological conversations and formation in local, public space as communities of healing on the margins.

all your soul and with all your strength and with all your mind; and Love your neighbor as yourself."[345] But like the privileged lawyer in this story, we want affirmation that the neighbors God wants us to love are people just like us. Many of our neighborhoods and local churches are homogenous and socially segregated.[346] "And who is my neighbor?" mirrors the question of our own hearts in this gospel narrative. Jesus answers by telling the Good Samaritan story and redefining "neighbor" as those people most *unlike* us, those people our own social circles reject as "other" or strangers or even enemies.[347] Jesus' answer causes us to *wonder* who these neighbors we are called to love might be in our own local neighborhoods.

A sense of inquisitiveness about our own community elicits questions about neighbors.[348] Whose stories have I never heard? Who have I *not* made room for in my life? Who am I relationally resistant to because of my own strong ideological beliefs or emotional, physical, and spiritual wounds? Whose presence is missing in my life, in my home, or in my church? Who are the people marginalized and oppressed in my own community or in my church? How do I get to know people who think and live differently from me? How do I get close enough to people so that I can listen to and learn from their stories? Wonderment begins with these prayerful questions of the heart with a humble poverty of spirit. Wonderment occurs in local contexts of homes and neighborhood streets, in places of business and in the institutions in our communities. God has moved into the neighborhood, and so we seek the divine Presence in strangely new places and in the faces of marginalized people in our communities. With curiosity, we seek to discover how to love God by loving neighbors who we have "othered."

---

345 Luke 10: 27.

346 Jennings, *After Whiteness*, pp. 6-7. Hegemony and homogeneity denote control; this must dramatically shift in theological spaces, says Jennings.

347 Luke 10: 25-37.

348 Bruce Maden, "God is in the Neighbourhood," *Spiritual Growth Ministries* (2006): p. 4, available online: https://www.sgm.org.nz/uploads/2/0/1/6/20165561/god_is_in_the_neighbourhood_-_bruce_maden.pdf; accessed February 23, 2022. Maden's research is given within the context of spiritual experience and spiritual formation in neighborhoods within community development settings.

After living 36 years in a neighborhood that I loved and where I knew everyone, I moved into a new home in my community in preparation for retirement. We prayed to be in a more diverse neighborhood where we could love our new neighbors. From my back bedroom window, I could see lights on in the Section 8 low-income housing units in the neighborhood where I walked daily. Across the street, I noticed the frequent police cars in the driveways, praying for my neighbors and wondering what pain might be hiding behind closed doors. Though I had a strong desire to invite neighbors over for coffee, I blamed my hesitancy on getting to know them on pandemic fatigue. I felt powerless to reach out to neighbors who were different from me, which was so opposite of how I had lived my life with intentional hospitality and an open door in the past. Stuck in a state of inertia, I began to reflectively wonder—about myself (What is going on with me?) and my neighbors (What are their stories?)

Maden suggests the need for "soul friends" (the Celtic idea of *anam cara*) in neighborhoods who can create a relational cultural climate in which neighbors can gradually become free of fear and more spiritually aware.[349] Creating a "culture of care" is conveyed through storytelling, according to Maden. This caring, interpersonal climate becomes a place of "nurture and safety, a sanctuary, for those who may have few other people to support them to become who they truly want to be."[350] Through storytelling and dialogue in safe spaces people share their experiences, ideas, resources, and spirituality. Over time, people's stories transform each other, and the community grows. In cultures of care, groups become a community and reach outwardly to care for the surrounding community.[351] Below the surface, deepest longings, dreams, desires for meaning in life, and "God moments" begin to emerge through the shared stories.[352]

---

349 Ibid., p. 5.; Aleshire, *Beyond Profession,* p. 124. Aleshire illuminates the idea of discernment companions and mentors as key for the cultivation of spiritual growth and maturity on life's journey, for "talking about their doubts and faith, and reflect on their fears and longings."

350 Ibid., p. 7.

351 Conde-Frazier, *Atando Cabos,* pp. 128; 71. Conde-Frazier believes that community members whose intent is to love God, neighbor, and creation are the community's theologians. Learning spaces in theological communities are places that welcome the Holy Spirit for communal discernment, listening, and sharing.

352 Ibid., pp. 7-8; Jennings, *After Whiteness,* p. 145. Jennings explains the creation of "personal, communal, storied" exchange networks that form friendships in a transformative imagined commu-

A group of girlfriends were coming over for a weekly Bible study and dis-
cussion in a course I was teaching entitled Peace Theology and Social Justice.
Feeling inner conflict about the subject matter I was teaching and my inept-
ness in loving my new neighbors, I welcomed my old, familiar friends into my
house. As I was closing my front door, I recognized my mail carrier who I had
smiled at and waved at all summer long from a distance. As she brought a box
to my porch, she asked me if I was a Christian. I replied yes. She asked me if I
taught Bible studies. I replied yes again. I invited her over for coffee after work
and Simone shared some of her story. I found out she was one of my neighbors
on the next street over where I walked daily. As we talked on the phone and
walked together in her neighborhood, we shared more of our stories about our
families, our vocations, and our struggles as women. Simone shared her desire
to study about the women in Exodus while making new friends. Our circles
of friendship converged to bring together our diverse stories through voices of
black and brown and white women that we both longed to listen to and learn
from. We sought to discover our own stories mirrored in the stories of scrip-
ture through the strong women of deliverance in the margins of the Exodus
liberation stories and to meet God as Liberator together. Simone became my
spiritual companion, my "soul friend" in my new neighborhood.[353]

Maden cited a randomly selected study of the general population of
Britain from twenty years ago in which 76% of the people studied admit-
ted to having a spiritual experience, yet only 6-8% of them attended an
institutional church regularly.[354] He explains that when safe space is created with freedom to question and freedom for expression, people share
experiences of "God moments" in their lives. Maden relates that "The
Spirit of Christ is seen as already in the neighbourhood, as already at the
heart of all that is and wanting to be noticed, embraced, and called forth.

---

nity. "Friendship is a real thing where people open their living to one another, allowing the paths
of life to crisscross in journeys imagined as in some sense shared," p. 147. Deep connection is
built up with reciprocity and mutuality.; Jordan, *Transforming Fire*, pp. 150-155. Though Jordan
focuses on a variety of "scenes of instruction," he points out the example of Jesus as storyteller as a
transformative model for us to learn from. pp. 15-22.

353 These stories are taken from over fifteen years of experience with DBS groups in various venues
that have multiplied organically through overlapping social networks in my community. Names,
identifying details and location have been changed to protect privacy.

354 Maden, "God is in the Neighbourhood, p. 9.

It is a perspective that challenges all to become and connect with what they already know and to enter into the reality that is already God in and around them."[355]

Since the Holy Spirit is ubiquitous, the secular world is the sacred place for spiritual activity to bring light, life, and healing as people encounter the spiritual realm amidst the brokenness that abounds where they live and move and have their being.[356] A robust view of the Holy Spirit affirms that God is already at work in the neighborhood. People become more conscious of the ultimate questions of life in their hearts, especially during times of dilemma or disturbances "when life events and transitions overflow the previous frame of mind that was able to contain them"[357] At these times, "soul friends," or spiritual companions, can ask reflective, noncoercive spiritual questions through natural conversations to help each other become more aware of the spiritual realities they are experiencing through reciprocal spiritual exploration. Maden gives examples of such questions. "What do you think is really going on here? What does this event mean for you? In the midst of this mess, what do you think is the best direction to take? If you were open to a divine Presence existing, what do you think that Presence would be saying to you now? From these experiences, what understandings are you developing about God or the Divine Presence?"[358] The Holy Spirit in the neighborhood moves in hidden and surprising ways to bring life, love, faith and hope to people seeking meaning and purpose in life. The spiritual journey is experienced more as a gradual, dynamic movement toward Jesus Christ, as the source of life, as an organic, alternative community is created among neighbors.

---

355 Ibid., p. 8.
356 Amos Yong, *Hospitality and the Other: Pentecost, Christian Practices, and the Neighbor* (Maryknoll, NY: Orbis Books, 2008), pp. 62-63.; Acts 17:28; Yong, *Renewing the Church*, p. 11. Throughout this book, Yong argues for a robust pneumatology in order to understand "church in its organic relationality and experiential spirituality."; Sun, *Attempt Great Things*, p. 27. Sun tells the story of Liu, the founder of the EFC (largely Chinese and Taiwanese) denomination as a model for how God uses ordinary people as partners with the Holy Spirit for finding others in need of healing within a community, like Jesus did.
357 Maden, "God is in the Neighbourhood, p. 10.
358 Ibid.

A group of Spanish-speaking friends were taking a marriage class together in a community building when suddenly a woman burst into the room, and emotionally began sharing about a disturbing dream she had the night before. Jacinta had heard a voice in the dream direct her to the community building to find a specific woman who would take her on a canoe down the "River of Life" where she would find safety and rest. She recognized the woman as the facilitator of the marriage class. "Where is the way to this River of Life?" the weeping woman desperately asked. Instead of continuing to teach the marriage class as planned, the facilitator opened up discussion in the group with all of the participants interacting together. Questions and eventually scriptures were explored to consider Jesus as the Way, the Truth, and the Life.

Spiritual formation begins organically as people discover truth together in places where a culture of care is cultivated through inclusive neighborly social interaction that supports spirituality as a journey—where spiritual awareness with questions and reciprocity of dialogue is encouraged through storytelling in safe, hospitable space where people naturally bond and belong.[359] The Spirit of God opens up space for glimpses of the miraculous in hospitable spaces of diversity that become places of peaceful refuge. Spiritual companions, and "persons of peace" in the neighborhood act as bridges for all people,[360] as heralds summoning neighbors with the good news that God's love is for everyone; everyone belongs to God![361]

Her inviting home was beautifully framed with a brick courtyard that her hard-working husband artfully created, complete with a trickling fountain beside an outdoor café table to greet neighbors in the mobile home park where she lived. The chocolate tres leches cake filled with strawberries was a favorite dessert at our GED class meetings in the community where I first met Nayeli. For two years her home was a welcoming place for las posadas *events at Christmas and sharing food from a local farm with neighbors. Her home was always filled with people and food as we sat on the stools around*

---

359 Yong, *Renewing the Church*, p. 117. Yong encourages a Spirit-led theological education where lifelong learners are created through ongoing, inclusive, dialogical conversations.
360 Watson and Watson, *Contagious Disciple Making*, p. 135. Watson and Watson describe three primary characteristics of "persons of peace." They are relationally open; they "hunger for spiritual answers for their deepest questions"; and they communicate what is learned with others.
361 Ibid., p. 18; Blumhardt, *Everyone Belongs to God*, p. 16.

her kitchen counter and watched her stirring arroz con leche *to share with us. One day Nayeli excitedly greeted us at her door to show us something she had built inside. As we walked in, we saw that she expanded her countertop table, making it wider with rounded corners with more seating and collapsible stools. Nayeli announced, "I want to make room for more people to come to our Friday night Discovery Bible Studies." I wept with joy to be considered one of her special guests in this sacred space as we "broke bread" with* panque y ponche, *feasting and remembering Jesus.*

Being and Acting: A Contemplative Discovery Approach to Scripture Reading with Neighbors

Hospitable space with spiritual companions and "persons of peace" facilitates storytelling, testimony, and dialogue with freedom for expression of life's questions. Spirituality grows inclusively and organically as love for God and love for neighbors among neighbors provides rich soil for seeds to grow roots deep and wide toward neighbors and upward toward the Light. As the ever-present Spirit reveals Jesus as alive in our neighborhoods, spiritual longing often leads these small alternative neighborhood communities to include ever widening and intersecting social circles of friends within a given locale, and even beyond. This *glocal* reach in our networked world can be rapidly expansive, especially in groups with diverse ethnicity where local friends share their spiritual stories across distances with family and friends around the globe.[362] Spiritual openness in a culture of care also often leads people with spiritual questions to a journey of discovery through the words of scripture to find Jesus as the Spirit reveals him as the Word made flesh and living among us.[363]

There are many ways available to read and interpret scripture, but one purpose of this book is to discover *spiritually formational* ways of reading scripture that leads to the *embodiment* of that contrasting Jesus Way in

---

362 Yong, *Renewing the Church,* p. 52. Yong describes how the church is evolving in a connected and networked world that is both local and global, or "glocal."
363 John 1: 1-18

contemporary society. It is a spiritually formational way that echoes *back* to remember the loving "ways of the Jesus Way" in our ancient origin story in Acts while pointing *forward* with hope and faith to a time when all will be fully restored in the future kingdom of God at the eschaton.[364] Green explains this embodied spiritual formation well by saying, "Scripture, read with and in the Spirit, actually works to conform us to Christ, materializing his character in us, incorporating us into his identity."[365]

The Discovery Bible Study (DBS) approach for reading scripture provides a framework that values storytelling, testimonials, and the formational study of scripture in the context of a hospitable culture of care for neighbors seeking to know God *through* scripture that is Spirit-led and focused to care for practical needs within the community itself and out in the larger society. The basic DBS framework[366] and its movement is modified and offered here as an experimental example, or creative remix that I have named, the Contemplative Discovery Approach (CDA). This approach is intended to guard against the potential dangers of purely literalist readings of scripture by providing a more contemplative posture for reading[367] with a more multi-layered, christotelic hermeneutic echoing patristic interpretation. In so doing, I hope to provide the means for a more loving embodied witness that points to Jesus as the Way in our world today, through noncoercive proclamation and through loving acts of mercy and justice for the common good in local neighborhoods. Stories are offered to illustrate the basic movement of DBS in each phase and the various ways such an approach might be experienced. Interlocutors will be parenthetically footnoted, so as not to interrupt the flow of movement

---

364 Aleshire, *Beyond Profession*, pp. 79 - 80. Aleshire, and all of the *Between the Times* authors, foresee that the future of theological education will need go beyond acquiring cognitive theological tools and must engage spiritual formation practices for deeper spiritual and moral reflection; theological education must be spiritually "formational."
365 Green, *Sanctifying Interpretation*, p. 126.
366 See Appendix A
367 Conde-Frazier, *Atando Cabos*, pp. 113- 118. Conde-Frazier hopes for a holistic hermeneutic that poses questions to the text that contemplatively engages readers' experiences by asking questions of the scriptures in ways where different angles are discerned by the community as illuminated by the Holy Spirit. In this process experience is interrogated through scripture in ways that critique and decolonize interpretations through diverse readings and inclusive reimagining.

in this approach. Descriptions of suggested modifications that follow each story are non-prescriptive. See Appendix A for the basic DBS components that I will be referring in categorical subheadings in my remix descriptions interspersed with exemplary stories. Appendix B delineates an abbreviated form of the Contemplative Discovery Approach I propose to facilitate greater accessibility and comprehension for practitioners.

TALK

For months, whenever the group was prompted to share about what they were thankful for or stressed out about, Randy shared his struggles with unemployment. Every week his story was told with increasing despair and futility. The whole group prayed for his family's needs and for him to get some interviews. An elderly lady in our group snuck the family an envelope with some money in it to help them out with bills. Each week we shared potluck meals to give single moms a break from cooking, and any leftover food was packed away for this family. The day came when Randy announced that our prayers for him were answered. He finally had an interview scheduled! As he shared his "thankful" testimony, Randy also humbly shared what was stressing him out about the interview. He did not have people who would write reference letters for him, and he didn't own a pair of pants that were appropriate for the type of interview he would be having. Carla thought her teenage son might have a pair of dress pants his size to share while a couple of other people offered to write him letters of reference. A community of care surrounded him with people who listened deeply to his story and offered the practical help needed in loving familial support.

One of the strengths of the DBS model is its "Talk" time. This time requires generous hospitality with enough time to honor and value everyone's story with freedom for expression. Optimally, this includes a space free from time constraints for deep, attentive listening. Personal storytelling is essential for communal spiritual formation that "breaks boundaries and crosses borders" through friendship.[368] The group members are

---

368 Jennings, *After Whiteness*, pp. 141; 148.

witnesses to each other's stories as they enter together into the scripture stories they will be reading. No one is forced into sharing their story, however, and all are free to refrain from talking if they wish.

"Talk" time would be further enhanced by the facilitator by starting meetings with a contemplative listening posture through a simple prayer of examen before people begin sharing. (See Appendix B). Storytelling prompts can be expanded beyond answering the standard questions about thankfulness and stressors in life, to more thought-provoking, noncoercive questions around narrative themes they will be encountering. When was a time in your life when you experienced deep love? Freedom? Fear? Awe? Healing? Suffering? Confusion? Questions about who needs help both within the community itself and in outside spheres of influence often come up naturally as a communal response during "Talk" time as group members respond to the needs presented.

[LOOK BACK (Session 2+)]

"Who told the story from last week to someone else this week?" the facilitator asked the group. One single mom named Emily said that she started telling her children the story about Jesus and the Samaritan woman at the well in parts throughout the week before bedtime and then they turned their questions about the passage into prayers. "What did this lady look like, Jesus?"; "Was she sad?"; "How did you know, Jesus, that she had so many husbands?" Emily said she was learning from her children how to ask childlike questions of wonder when she prayed with them instead of giving her children all the answers.

This part of DBS flows naturally from the previous section and the two sections could be combined since both involve testimony and storytelling. Listening to testimonial stories gives hope and faith about the reality of God and that the realities in life can be transformed in surprising ways because of God's loving presence alive in the real life stories of people—just like in scripture.[369] Honor for each person's story or testimo-

---

369 Day, *Notes of a Native Daughter,* pp. 1-3.

ny can be offered by a short space of sacred silence, the *silencio* of *lectio divina,* between storytellers. Some may choose to enter into silent prayer of intercession or thanksgiving during this time. Praying aloud is neither forced, assumed, nor expected. The specific "culture of prayer"—the specific form prayer becomes—eventually emerges from within the group itself in all of its diverse expression. Some groups remain in silence, others might recite a familiar liturgical prayer, others pray in various tongues or languages or in fervent intercessory prayer, and sometimes any of the above occur in the same group. No effort is made to control the form that prayer becomes within a group—it just happens within the prayer culture of the people themselves.

READ and RETELL

The day arrived for our first "neighborhood" gathering where the social circles of my "soul friend," Simone, and my own converged. Everyone was gracious and excited to meet each other and since two of the people lived in California, we decided to use a hybrid format, which would also allow us to continue even locally because of the pandemic to come. After a lengthy storytelling time that helped us to get to know each other since many of us were strangers to one another, the brief passage from Exodus about the midwives was read aloud slowly, first in English and then in Spanish, in order to honor the heart languages of all the women who were present. After the passage was read aloud, the group was invited to "retell" the story. Since all the women in the group shared during storytelling time that they were church attenders, it was pretty predictable that they would have a hard time retelling the story without summarizing the "moral of the story" or personalizing it to explain what it meant to them. The facilitator prompted, "Retell the story in your own words." As predicted, one lady shared what the story meant in her life. Without shutting the first lady down, the facilitator rephrased the prompt, "Retell the story as if you were there watching the whole thing happen." One of the Black sisters said she would give it a try. The story came to life through the natural way the story was expressed as if it were happening before our very eyes as we re-entered the scene together and saw the story transform with a new perspective that disrupted and reoriented the way the story unfolded. Quite gradually, as this gifted sister retold the Exodus stories with her unique voice, each of the women found greater freedom to voice these stories in her own culturally distinct language and perspective for the enrichment and enjoyment of everyone present.

The reading and retelling phase of DBS is when attention to the scripture narrative begins. Depending on the literacy levels of the group and the languages spoken, the passage can be followed along by reading as one person reads aloud (or several in multiple languages), or the group can just listen. In a *lectio divina* style remix, this phase lends itself to an imaginative contemplation of the scripture as it is read aloud.[370] In this *lectio* portion as the scripture is read aloud, listeners would be asked contemplative prompts and questions such as, "Imagine yourself in this scene as it is read aloud. What do your senses see, hear, smell, taste, and feel? Notice if you identify with a particular character in the scene or are just an observing bystander. What emotions, body sensations and thoughts do you experience as the story unfolds?" Imaginative contemplation during *lectio* (reading) would facilitate retelling the scripture narrative from various perspectives while staying on script and lessening the tendency toward "sermonizing" about meaning.[371] Stories could be retold in first person, dramatized, or even artistically expressed through drawing the scene and then explaining it through pictures.[372]

READ and LOOK

(Part 1) The first day a passionate young man named Ricardo with fiery black eyes joined our Discovery Bible Study for ESL and GED students. He entered the room announcing, "I don't believe in God, and I have no interest

370 Calhoun, *Spiritual Disciplines Handbook,* pp. 187-190. Calhoun describes traditional *lectio divina* in its entirety here.
371 Conde-Frazier, *Atando Cabos,* p. 117. Conde-Frazier affirms the wisdom and draw of mystical traditions of spirituality for the younger generations as possible areas of exploration for the future church and theological institutions.
372 Jordan, *Transforming Fire,* pp. 15-27; pp. 150-156. Jordan encourages creative approaches for theological instruction.

in church. I'm just here to be with my friends." Not fazed, we began with the stories in Genesis. After reading the creation story in Genesis, the facilitator asked the question, "What does this passage tell us about God?" The answer that Ricardo gave stood out, "God is generous, and his gifts are good." More questions began to percolate as he continued wrestling with scriptures. The story about Cain and Abel noticeably shook him up. After this story when the facilitator asked, "What does this passage tell us about people?" his answer was an interesting one. "I think I know what the original sin was: people were never meant to kill animals. We were designed to be vegetarians. Killing of animals is the original sin. Abel shouldn't have killed the lamb, but Cain shouldn't have killed his brother. Killing is wrong." The facilitator encouraged him to keep asking God questions as more stories unfolded over the next nine months to discover whether his hypothesis was true.

When the story of Abraham and Isaac came up, Ricardo was incredulous. "How could a father ever kill his son even if a voice from heaven told him to? He would have no love! Why would God ask him to do such a horrible thing?" His struggle with killing and with blood continued through the selected Old Testament narratives about animal sacrifices in Leviticus and the killing of people in other stories. The facilitator exercised restraint in giving pat answers to lessen the struggle and to defend God's actions, instead trusting that the Holy Spirit was working in the midst of the conflicts in these narratives yet wondering how the angst was affecting the rest of the group who often added their own questions or responded with uncertainty. Still, Ricardo continued coming. (To be continued in next section...)

In the Read and Look phase of DBS, the scripture passage is read again, and a simple question is asked, "What does this say about God (or Jesus)?" This phase of DBS (and the next one facilitated by the question about what the passage says about people) tends toward a literalist reading which can be problematic, especially in the Old Testament narratives. One positive thing is that even a literalist reading encourages people to wrestle with the texts. The negative outcome, however, is its potential for leaving people at any given point with a skewed or "unworthy" image of the character/nature of God being violent, unloving, angry, wrathful, or capricious. Although a *literal* view is one valuable layer for scripture interpretation, and the two questions about God's character and nature (and humanity's character and nature in the next section) are valuable to ask and wrestle through, the tendency toward a purely *literalist*[373] interpretation can be lessened or even avoided by adding the *spiritual sense* of patristic interpretation in later contemplative readings in this model—the allegorical, moral, and anagogical layers of patristic interpretation—through contemplative questions.

A DBS remix of the Read and Look phase would begin with this first layer of reading for literal meaning through *lectio divina*. As the *meditatio* reading begins, *both* DBS questions are asked for consideration through meditation. What does this passage say about the character and nature of God (or Jesus)? What does this passage say about the character and nature of people (or humanity)? Jersak quotes N.T. Wright's helpful, open question for this literal reading of the text which directs the listener to consider context and genre: "What does this text intend to refer to, and *how* does it intend to refer to it?"[374] Williams suggest noticing a text's movement; where is the text moving the reader to? "What is the text as a full unit trying not to say or to deny?"[375] For additional questions about God or people that elicit perspectives through the voices of the oppressed or marginalized people in the scripture passage see Appendix C. This results in

---

373 Jersak, *A More Christlike Word*, pp. 113-125. Jersak distinguishes between a *literalist* interpretation and the *literal* reading of scripture in the patristic sense. Jersak summarizes the *literalist* view: "In short, *biblical literalism* and *inerrancy* predetermine limits on what the Bible cannot do or say before even reading the text or allowing it to speak for itself." Without careful attention to genre, metaphor, historical and cultural context, the *literalist* reads the "bare letters" as "the Bible clearly says." A patristic *literal* interpretation is the first layer of reading that "asks the text what it is doing" and takes into consideration genre, metaphor, historical and cultural context. The literal sense is the "launching pad on to the moral (tropological), and spiritual (gospel, typological) reading of the Bible," p. 115.

374 Jersak, *A More Christlike Way*, p. 119. Jersak quotes N.T Wright, "A Conversation with N.T. Wright: What Do You Mean by 'Literal'?" interview by Dr. Peter Enns, The BioLogos Foundation, September 8, 2010, video, 4:29, https://youtu.be/fxQpFosrTUk.

375 Rowan Williams, "The Bible Today: Reading and Hearing," in *Transcript from the Larkin-Stuart Lecture at a special joint Convocation of Trinity and Wycliffe colleges in Toronto, Canada* (April 16, 2007), p. 1-5; available online: https://rowanwilliams.archbishopofcanterbury.org/articles.php/2112/the-bible-today-reading-hearing-the-larkin-stuart-lecture.html; accessed March 1, 2022.
John 14:6.

a discussion that is facilitated, *not taught or answered*, by the facilitator. All are invited, but not forced, to participate through discussion. Everyone's participation is affirmed, and discoveries about what the passage says about God and people are derived communally and summarized by the facilitator.[376] This affirms what the Holy Spirit is specifically teaching *through* the scriptures *through* the specific gathered community.[377] Other components of the patristic *literal sense* (textual criticism, genre analysis, and lexical exegesis) will be addressed in the last DBS phase.

READ and LOOK AGAIN

(Part 2) The group finally entered into the New Testament narratives nine months later. Memorably, during the storytelling time before the scripture reading, Ricardo, for the first time asked to share his story from his youth in Mexico. Ricardo was a teenager when his girlfriend got pregnant, and both of their families kicked them out of their homes, so they lived underneath a tree in their town. After work one day, he found her bleeding from the pregnancy that wasn't full term yet. He called their family members to try to get a ride to the hospital, but no one would help them. He picked her bleeding body up into his arms and carried her the whole distance to the hospital. In the emergency room, the baby was delivered. Ricardo held his stillborn son and his girlfriend, still bloody from birth, in his arms. Wordless, our whole group held his tragic pain with silence. The veil was being drawn to get a glimpse into some of the reasons, perhaps, that these scripture stories about blood and loss and violence between family members were being experienced in such a traumatic way and with such angst within his heart.

---

376   Green, *Sanctifying Interpretation,* p. 127. Green highlights the Good Samaritan story in Luke 10:26 where Jesus asked, "What do the Scriptures say and how do you read them?" Green explains,"... Jesus graces us by directing us to the Scriptures, pressing us into the work of interpretation, which begins bit by bit somehow to lay bare the secrets of our heart." The stories work on our hearts as all people participate in the work of interpretation.

377   Jersak, *A More Christlike Word,* p. 122. "...The Scriptures claim the necessity of illumination by the Spirit and the gospel of Jesus to remove veils over our hearts and eyes that would otherwise obscure God's message."

Almost apologetically, the facilitator directed the group to the scripture passage for the day: the crucifixion story of Jesus. Heartbroken, she wrestled in her own heart as she carried both the story of Ricardo's suffering and the story of Jesus' suffering with tension, praying for the Holy Spirit to be Teacher and to bring life and revelation to the heaviness in the room. Would this young man, and all the other tender hearts present, see the crucifixion as an act of wrathful violence by God the Father putting his son to death in such a cruel and bloody way on the cross? How can God's actions be defended or portrayed as somehow loving in such a violent scene of scripture?

After the story was read aloud, the facilitator stalled, reversing the order of the questions asked, "What does this crucifixion passage say about people?" The answer was voiced unanimously by the group, "People can be heartless and violent for all kinds of reasons. People can betray and abandon and fear each other." Then the next question was asked, "What does this passage say about God?" Silence. The facilitator had experienced how the Spirit often worked mysteriously in the awkwardness of silence, allowing for deep reflection, so she prayerfully waited. She just couldn't bear to lock eyes with Ricardo, but it was his voice she heard answering the question through his tears, as she waited for the interpreter to translate. "The Father was holding his suffering Son as he bled on the cross. The Father's heart was bleeding with pain too as his Son died in his arms. All Jesus ever had was love for people. His Father knew that and embraced his Son with love as he died because our violence killed him." Holy silence.

The Read and Look Again phase of DBS can be entirely remixed to elicit the *spiritual sense* (the allegorical, moral, and anagogical layers) in the next reading of scripture through contemplative questions.[378] As the scripture is read aloud this time, the facilitator elicits questions which become prayers asking for a revelation of Christ through scripture by the Holy Spirit's in the *oratio* of *lectio divina*. A question leading to a spiritual

---

378 Jersak, *A More Christlike Word*, p. 135. Jersak's christotelic question, or the patristic interpretation's allegorical sense, affirms that "all Scripture points to Jesus Christ and his gospel, or we are misinterpreting and misusing it." Green also points out Lubac's historical medieval exegesis in this quote, "Jesus Christ brings about the unity of Scripture because he is the endpoint and fullness of Scripture. Everything in it is related to him. In the end he is its sole object. Consequently, he is, so to speak, its whole exegesis…" Lubac quoted in Green, *Sanctifying Interpretation*, p. 131

sense of scripture that is christotelic and allegorical might be: How does this passage reveal or point to Christ and his gospel?[379] Another question can be used to discern the polyphony of spiritual voices present in the text. Where do you hear the voice of self-giving love and life in this story? (Or to contrast, where do you hear the voice of the accuser that comes to steal, kill, and destroy?)[380] Next, a moral question might be posed such as Jersak's questions: "How will this passage nourish my growth as a follower of Jesus Christ? That is, 'How will it transform me so that the truth of my being (the image of Christ) becomes the way of my being (the likeness of Christ)?"[381] A receptive listening posture makes room for spiritual revelation of Christ through scripture that leads to transformative change within human hearts.[382] These questions might become invitations for loving God and loving neighbors in specific ways as participants discuss what these questions in the passage prompted for change within their own hearts.[383] How scriptures are read matters. As scripture is read contemplatively, the Spirit works within us *through* scripture. As the texts are prayerfully wrestled through, people are spiritually formed and transformed.[384]

INSIDE ME

It was another rainy, dreary day in Cleveland, Ohio as we met inside the sparsely furnished building with concrete walls painted gray. Sarah, the ESL teacher didn't feel like teaching English, much less staying after class for the

---

379 Ibid. This question could be used for both Old Testament texts and kingdom of God parables and stories.

380 Ibid., pp. 204-206.

381 Ibid., p. 132.

382 Green, *Sanctifying Interpretation*, p. 130. Green explains that a Pentecostal hermeneutic stimulates reflection as people come "to the Scriptures expecting to encounter *Christ;* and second, they came to the Scriptures to *encounter* Christ."

383 Green, *Sanctifying Interpretation*, p. 126. Green states, "...Scripture, read with and in the Spirit, actually works to conform us to Christ, materializing his character in us, incorporating us into his identity."

384 Ibid., pp. 126-129.; Aleshire, *Beyond Profession*, p. 123. Aleshire contends that scripture is an invitation for spiritual formation, not simply for study. He states, "This invitation will require the prompting of the professor, the willingness of the student to live into the text, and sufficient time for students to let the text stir their souls."

Discovery Bible study but pushed through for some reason anyway. She couldn't help but notice the enthusiasm of the rest of the group as they discussed their insights about the beauty of the creation story in the first chapter of Genesis, but her heart still felt dull and lifeless inside. After the scripture discussion the facilitator asked this question, "According to this study, what are you doing well and what do you need to change?" Sarah couldn't think of anything she was doing well and didn't really want to think of anything that needed change. But she kept hearing one phrase from the scripture passage resounding as a refrain in her heart, over and over again, "God saw that it was good.... God saw that it was good..." She couldn't deny the gentle Spirit's voice of life speaking into her heart, changing her interior dullness and opening her eyes to see the gray, cloudy day outside as "good" from God's perspective. She considered what it might mean for her to daily practice seeing something in creation as simple as Cleveland weather as "good"—a gift from God. Something inside was changing her perspective.

This part of the DBS process brings the focus inward to self-evaluate spiritual formation by asking questions designed to bring about repentance or behavioral change. The tendency with the original prompts is that they can foster an overly active inner critic that performs to please God. Instead, this last movement can be the final *contemplatio* part of *lectio divina,* where each person is invited to rest in the presence of God with the reality that the Spirit is bringing about transformation through *theosis.*[385] In that place of rest, there might be a specific sense of what might be changing in their heart. Resting in the peace of God also may bring about contemplation of the anagogical sense of the scriptures to remember with hope that our present realities have "eternal significance, leading us toward our true homeland.[386] God is restoring all things beginning now *within* us and also *through* us. A final discussion can be offered around the questions: "What do you sense the Spirit is changing in your heart? How does the Spirit seem to be moving us communally to engage

---

385 Luu, *Jesus of the East,* p. 141. Luu describes the *theosis* of the early Eastern fathers as transformative growth into the likeness of God. "They saw that people needed to grow into their true selves, understood that sin had made people sick, both spiritually and physically, and believed that people needed healing and liberation." p. 157.; Delay, *The Wild Land Within,* p. 31.
386 Jersak, *A More Christlike Word,* p. 131.

the community in which we live?" Green encapsulates this movement in his words describing spiritual formation through scripture. "By the Spirit's grace, the Scripture works salvation, renewing our vision of the world by transforming us at the depths of our being. So transformed, we begin to discover our place in the mission of God entrusted to the church, and to bring goodness and justice to bear in the lives of our neighbors and enemies."[387]

WHO ELSE?

One of our Discovery groups in particular had a heart for the unhoused people in our community who typically spent their time around picnic tables in our city square. We had met there regularly together the summer before, sharing bagged lunches and engaging folks in conversation. But now it was nearing Christmas and the deep snow, and the cold northeast Ohio wind had kept us from spending time outside in the cold with these neighbors. Joe had heard a rumor that the local business owners around the city square had complained about being harassed for food, money, and shelter by our neighbors who were in need of these things, and so the police had an order forbidding them from loitering in the square. We decided as a group to spend our Christmas Eve with these marginalized neighbors as a peaceful protest and demonstration of love.

This humble and self-giving group, many of whom were living in poverty themselves, festively decorated the picnic tables overflowing with cheese and crackers, ham and mashed potatoes, green beans with bacon, and an assortment of pies and brightly decorated Christmas cookies that their children made. Since nobody else was in the city square dazzling with Christmas lights, Joe led the rest of us out into the neighboring streets to find and invite our guests. As we reunited with our friends, the tables turned into a feast through laughter, warmth, and food as we all shared Christmas memories and thoughts about the Christmas story. It wasn't too long before we were approached by a policeman who was familiar with some of the faces around our table. Pointing to several of our neighbors, he told the rest of us that they weren't permitted to be

---

387 Green, *Sanctifying Interpretation*, p. 127.

in the city square. Joe spoke up, "But we invited these friends to join us for our Christmas Eve picnic. Would you like to join us too, officer?" The policeman quietly said, "Merry Christmas," and turned and walked away.

Often, ideas for communal action come at the end of the DBS time, through the desires prompted within the scripture story itself as to how to engage marginalized people or the injustices that the scripture story mirrors in the local community. As we enter into *incarnatio*, our own need for healing and reconciliation with other people often comes into view. With vulnerability and compassion, the healing that begins in the small group transformed through scripture begins to expand hearts with love into the larger community in need of collective trauma healing.[388] When considering the DBS questions about who else needs to hear the story or be invited to study with the group, we can reframe it without a sense of "us/them" or "lost/saved" categories. A revision of these questions for a more inclusive collective wholeness might be: "Who else might be longing for healing together with us through scripture and community? What neighborhoods are calling us to stand in solidarity with them as Jesus would? What healing, reconciliation, or recovery can we be contributors to for restoration in our local community?"

In Western contexts, group participants usually begin to share widely accessible resources (books, podcasts, online sermons and courses, liturgy/lectionary Bible apps etc.) for deeper spiritual exploration, providing additional background pertaining to the genre, history, and cultural contexts of the scriptures studied. Quite naturally, some participants begin asking about where people in the group attend traditional institutional churches in the community. Connectivity is encouraged by the facilitator and group participants beyond the DBS spiritual formation community

---

388 Luu, *Jesus of the East*, p. 186. Luu relates that "When we are isolated and alone, it is difficult to touch and see these wounds, but within communities of healing we can receive these reminders and testimonies. These are communities not only of the wounded, but also of healers who wish to love, accept, and form covenants with the wounded." Communities of healing can provide a venue for collective trauma healing.; Delay, *The Wild Land Within*, pp. 145-179.; Holmes, *Crisis Contemplation*, pp. 13; 34.

as those who long to connect and grow within a larger historically-rooted spiritual community express that desire.[389]

As the DBS concludes, the group is encouraged to be attentive to the way the story continues to come alive throughout the week, in ordinary and extraordinary ways. Each person is reminded to continue reflecting on the scripture story and to share it with others as the Spirit's invitation is noticed in everyday life. Shared facilitation begins shortly after groups begin to gather together. After the approach is modeled for a few weeks, anyone can take turns facilitating by simply asking the given questions. This is encouraged so that group structure remains flat and non-hierarchical, spiritual gifts are recognized and practiced, and groups multiply.[390] Open, inclusive groups with ever-expanding and overlapping networks of loving care and friendship with neighbors, strangers, and enemies organically grow and multiply as the love of God, prompted by the Spirit of God, demonstrates that Jesus is alive *as* the Way, and *in* the followers of the Jesus Way, where we live. Williams relates that the process of reading scripture theologically has life-giving effects:

> Ultimately, Scripture brings us back to the uniquely creative moment of God's freedom—to the grace of a free bestowal that can create what is other and then, by love and welcome, transform that other into a sharer and communicator of the same joyful, generative act. 'The word of life...[that]we have seen and heard we declare to you, so that you and we together may share in a common life, that life which we share with the Father and the Son Jesus Christ' (1 John 1:1-3)."[391]

---

389 Heath, *God Unbound*, p. 59.

390 Jennings, *After Whiteness*, p. 141. Jennings envisions shared facilitation in order to "place oneself in the journey of others" with "the vulnerability of a centeredness from below."

391 Rowan Williams, "The Bible Today," pp. 1-5.

We can look toward the future with hope and faith that loving God and loving our neighbor in these small ways has the potential to transform our neighborhoods into peaceful, beloved communities.

SUMMARY

The research in this book began as a quest for discovering a more Christ-like approach for contemplative scripture reading that might unite diverse neighbors in an embodied spirituality that could promote local peace. I began my search by exploring the ancient history of the Jesus movement. By first focusing on Jesus who referred to himself as the Way,[392] and his namesake followers who were also called the Way,[393] I noted that it was their *manner* of life—their *approach* to living with each other and with neighbors—that defined them as such.

Jesus, as the Way, enfleshed his calling to preach good news to the poor, to bring freedom and sight to the blind, and to set the oppressed free by bringing God's loving favor in visible and tangible ways to people through healing, storytelling, discussion, miracles, and ritual in various scenes of instruction. His "Way" was *love*, expressed and embodied. Jesus reinterpreted sacred script by pointing to himself as the fulfillment of every law and prophetic utterance to demonstrate that every word of God breathed Love. Subversively through his Sermon on the Mount teachings, Jesus lived that *Way* as a marginalized Jew—as Word made flesh—among marginalized people with disenfranchised disciples as his family. He disrupted social and religious paradigms by loving neighbors, including neighbors that were considered enemies. Jesus' ultimate expression of self-giving, co-suffering, radically forgiving love was not a sermon; it was embodied on the cross. His resurrection made real the promised hope for the restoration of life for all people. At Pentecost, the life-giving Spirit rebirthed children of God to continue the Jesus Way forward in diverse contexts.

By the Spirit, the Way of Jesus spiritually transformed this diverse family into the Jesus Way, proclaiming good news and living it out in the margins of Roman society. They gathered together as an alternative,

---

392 John 14:6.
393 Acts 9:2; Acts 19:9, 23; Acts 24:14, 22.

contrasting family within the context of patriarchal Roman Empire. The Jesus Way was a beloved community of practice. As the diverse new family gathered in homes, their communal spiritual practices broke social, ethnic, religious and gender barriers. Remembering Jesus, they devotedly shared a common life, apostolic teaching, the breaking of bread, and prayer.[394] Remembering his way of love, they tangibly loved, served, and shared with local neighbors in contrast with the pervasive violence, violation, and domination of their society. In loving neighbors, they loved God. As the gospel of love was proclaimed and embodied among neighbors through the Jesus Way, new gatherings formed as they multiplied and scattered geographically—and as they were further marginalized and persecuted.

Cultural moments in history have a scattering effect on the Jesus Way. As Jesus followers began to inhabit new spaces, their inclusive hospitable gatherings became a refuge, a place of belonging. As they reached out in practical love to care for the poor, sick and dying, God's love took on flesh through them to extend beyond their social boundaries. As the Jesus Way demonstrated a liberation of social, gender, ethnic, and class differences in society, their "ways" were a prophetic dissent to speak truth to the power of Empire. Gradually, as the Church continued to grow in the fourth century following Constantine's conversion, institutionalization began to mirror the political hierarchy and authority of the Roman Empire, shifting the Jesus Way as a religion of the powerless to a religion of power. A minority voice arose as prophetic dissent through the desert saints as a protest in the margins to penetrate the numbness of history to re-express the former Jesus Way, revitalizing the way of love for God and love for neighbor. This historical pattern of tension between order and prophecy, the pastoral and the apostolic, institutional maintenance and transformative movement for change can be observed through various groups of disciples who were "outliers" in the margins throughout Christian history. Most often the prophetic minority voices were ignored, controlled, or persecuted; however, this pattern of tension created revitalizing forward momentum of scattering and gathering that resulted in new forms of spir-

---

394 Acts 2:42-47.

itual practice calling into remembrance the embodied spirituality of love that was their origin story.

Cultural moments of collective crisis, even pandemics, change history. Evidence was given from the first centuries that the early followers of Jesus embodied love at such times by selflessly serving with solidarity the sick and dying. They cared in tangible ways for neighbors and enemies in the midst of cultural crisis. Times of crisis precipitate faith crises when people begin to ask questions of theodicy in the midst of suffering. The concurrent crises give birth to spiritual revitalization movements through collective action as a response.

One such contemporary theological response during the present crises of pandemic and societal strife, is the *Theological Education Between the Times* book series, that gathered a diverse group of scholars to collaborate for "critical theological conversations about the meanings and purposes of theological education in a time of deep change."[395] In summary, with regard to spiritual formation, this group sees that the Jesus Way forward for the church (through the training of faith leaders) includes deep ways of *belonging* including: visible relational connection that is embodied with inclusive, multidimensional gatherings joining diverse voices for collaboration with mutuality and reciprocity. Future formats will include online/virtual communities, exchange networks, cohorts, mobile groups, and contemplative and creative spaces. Ways of *being* are spiritually formational in focus and are described as communal, fluid, Spirit-led, life-giving, dialogical, and decolonized. Formats would include storytelling, asking questions, reenacting narratives and testimonials with deep listening and communal interpretation alongside mature mentors to center spiritual virtues and ethics. Ways of *acting* must align theology with practice, orthodoxy with orthopraxy. Local dialogues and enactment through social justice activism, mercy initiatives, and compassionate solidarity have global reach for speaking truth to power, to turn the tables on unjust systems of oppression, and to bring collective trauma healing to society. These ways of belonging, being, and acting echo back to former ways of embod-

---

395 Smith, *Theological Education*, quote from inside the series' book covers.

ied expression of the Way while embracing twenty-first century cultural realities and technologies.

As the center of Christianity on our planet shifted to the Global South and East a generation ago, the transcendent voice of God prophesies to the Christianity of power in the West through the "poor, the hungry, the persecuted, and even the dehumanized"[396] brothers and sisters in Africa, Latin America, and Asia. The rapid expansion of the Jesus Way in the Global South and East is mostly indigenous and more organic in its reach. Disciple Making Movements (DMMs) differ from the expressions in the West in that they are characterized by an egalitarian approach representative of the ethnic, racial, and economic classes of the local context. Ecclesiology is flattened and is primarily a layperson movement through relational networks. Pentecostalization is unlike the prosperity gospel in the West. Indigenous worldviews support supernatural signs and wonders present in scripture narratives. Suffering, exile, oppression, and persecution are relevant to people in the Global South and East, so these scripture themes are accessible and relatable. Scripture narratives are engaged, proclaimed, and embodied locally. In organic DMMs, Jesus Christ is followed by lovingly obeying scripture without specific outside structures and forms to help or organize groups of followers. It is a Spirit-empowered kingdom of God movement that multiplies, proclaiming the love of God to neighbors that they too belong to God.

One prominent approach for spiritual formation in organic DMMs is Discovery Bible Study (DBS). This approach is communal, accessible, and reproducible. DBS gatherings are typically small, hospitable, and home-based. Storytelling and testimonies are honored, and scripture stories are engaged through questions, meditated upon, reenacted and retold. Everyone participates as the facilitator guides through questions, without teaching, as participants wrestle with scripture together. The Holy Spirit is considered the Teacher in DBS groups, and the effect is a decolonized gospel reading within the local cultural context. Participants are encouraged

---

396 Jenkins, *The Next Christendom,"* p. 256.

to share the scripture stories with others and to practice the transformative truths that the Holy Spirit illuminates personally to them.

This grassroots approach to spiritual formation fulfills most of the predictions of the *Theological Education Between the Times* scholarly voices. Spiritual formation using DBS is communal, relationally connected, and Spirit-led. Since all people participate, mutuality and reciprocity of diverse voices occurs are deeply listened to through wrestling with spiritual questions, storytelling, and respectful reflection as texts decolonize through indigenous voices in the local culture. Power differentials are flattened through egalitarian participation. Spiritual transformation occurs over time personally and through networks of exchange. Stories are reenacted and embodied through various scenes of instruction in the community with invitations to include others as social circles of influence mobilize and converge. Compassionate action, congruent with the scripture narratives, is encouraged and embodied with family, friends, and neighbors. The historic spiritual practices of the Jesus Way (a common life, apostolic instruction, prayer, and the breaking of bread) exist in local, organic expressions of DMMs. Western tendencies toward literalist interpretations of scripture and reliance on information through teachers, and perhaps discomfort with pentecostalization effects may be potential barriers for implementing this approach in Western contexts. A posture of intellectual and spiritual humility is necessary to listen to and learn from the Global South and East voices who prophesy of better ways of engaging our marginalized neighbors in the West through spiritual formation practices that could be the Jesus Way of the future.

If the Global South and East speak to the West today for the revitalization of spiritual formation for the Church, then the *value* for ancient spiritual practices must be recovered too. Radical hospitality that values and loves our most marginalized neighbors must be extended by "taking the church to the edge rather than seeking to bring the margin to the center."[397] Disciplemaking must occur at sites where we segregate so our stories enfold to form a common life that is not homogenous, but

---

397 Flunder, *Where the Edge Gathers*, p. 131.

authentically inclusive, celebrating our mutuality enriched by relational reciprocity. Dominant tables must be abandoned for people to become listening and learning guests at unfamiliar tables. Feasting together at such tables transcends everyday toils and the futility of life to celebrate the love of God for all. Sacred space is decolonized and reoriented to center Jesus as the Feast. By remembering his cruciform self-giving love, we re-member our dis-membered world by eating bread and drinking wine at a wide open table—an inclusive love feast—to toast with prophetic defiance, and with a faithful enactment today, the reality of a future kingdom of love where everything will one day be fully restored.

Ancient scripture interpretation for a more "apostolic instruction" must also be valued and recovered. Scripture is like a mirror through which we encounter the love of God and ourselves. The Bible reveals Jesus as its center through a christotelic hermeneutic in which all scripture finds its consummation in Christ. This gospel-focused message is liberative. Through scripture, we struggle together with God, and we are transformed together by the Spirit's transfiguring work of theosis. In the wrestling, peacemakers make peace with scriptures through the discovery that Christ not only reconciles the confusing and conflicting texts but is the Reconciler of our confusing and conflicting relationships with neighbors, even our enemy-neighbors. Spiritual transformation takes place *through* the scriptures and *through* our neighbors by the Spirit of love. A multi-layered, patristic scripture hermeneutic facilitates a christocentric lens of love that encourages the embodiment of that love for God and love for neighbor. Scripture read in this "Emmaus Way"[398], unveils Jesus and his gospel as the revelatory fulfillment of the Law and the Prophets. The earliest apostolic instruction among Jesus followers modeled this way of scripture interpretation. As the literal (genre, cultural context, historical) and spiritual senses (allegorical, moral, anagogical) of the text are contemplated, there is a discovery of the "good" whereby followers "bring the peace of God to bear on the world."[399]

---

398 Jersak, *A More Christlike Word*, p. 28.
399 Green, *Sanctifying Interpretation*, p. xiii.

Interpreting scripture for apostolic instruction requires a meditative prayer posture, similar to the spiritually formative *lectio divina* approach for reading scripture which was predominant for the first 1500 years of church history. Beginning with silence, the movements of *lectio divina* involve reading scripture, meditating on scripture, praying through scripture, and resting contemplatively with scripture. The polyphony of spiritual voices of sacrificial religion can also be distinguished for the voice of self-giving love when scripture is read with a contemplative posture. The ancient spiritual practices of radical hospitality at open inclusive tables on the margins, a patristic hermeneutic for reading scripture, and a contemplative prayer posture and practice must be recovered for authentic spiritual formation. A patristic hermeneutic guards against literal*ist* scripture interpretation and goes beyond gaining information *about* scripture to being transformed *through* scripture. Contemplative prayer practices faithfully facilitate personal and communal illumination through the Holy Spirit as a means for relationally and ethically embodying a love-ethic with neighbors.

In our present cultural moment, a "corporate dark night of the soul"[400] enables a liberating love for neighbors, a sense of curiosity about life's deepest questions, and a longing to seek "soul friends" in neighborhoods. As spiritual questions are pondered through neighborly conversations, cultures of care are gradually created outside of traditional churches in grassroots communities. Since the Holy Spirit is present everywhere, spiritual longing, and then formation begins to grow in homes and public spaces in local neighborhoods. Eventually, neighbors seek deeper spiritual conversations, Spirit-led connections are made, and a desire to read scripture together occurs organically as neighbors engage followers embodying the Jesus Way.

A Contemplative Discovery Approach was offered as a spiritual formation experiment for revitalizing the Church in the West as a means for loving neighbors in ways that promotes peace among them in local

---

400 Heath, *The Mystic Way*, p. 10.

neighborhoods.[401] The strengths of the Discovery Bible Study used in Disciple Making Movements were integrated with a recovery of ancient spiritual practices of contemplative prayer, scripture interpretation, and radical hospitality. This experimental approach for spiritual formation was described in detail and illustrated through stories from my experiences in organic grassroots groups over the last fifteen years and was abbreviated in Appendix B. In hospitable settings and through neighborly storytelling, contemplative reading, and Spirit-led interpretation of scriptures, stories about God and about us are mirrored and then embodied locally in decolonized ways. Spiritual transformation through the contemplative reading of scripture and a multi-layered patristic interpretive approach is embodied within a culture of mutual care among neighbors and then led by the Spirit into the community to love neighbors with a love for God birthed *through* scriptures that spiritually transformed them. By focusing on hospitable practices in marginalized neighborhoods on a *local* scale, possibilities for the embodiment of love for God and neighbor through compassionate action and *small* scale justice initiatives can be reimagined for specific communities to foster peace for the local common good. Through the reality of our highly connected, networked, and globalized world—and the life-giving, movement of the Holy Spirit—local efforts for kingdom of God peacebuilding have surprising, global reach.[402]

---

401 John Paul Lederach, "Cultivating Peace: A Practitioner's View of Deadly Conflict and Negotiation," in *Contemporary Peacemaking: Conflict, Violence and Peace Processes,* ed. John Darby and Roger MacGinty (New York: Palgram Macmillan, 2003), p. 34-35. As a veteran peacebuilder, Lederach uses "the metaphor of cultivator more than harvester, towards nourishment of soil and plant more than picking the fruit. The images that accompany this complementary metaphor suggest an organic connection to context, the building of relationships, and a commitment to process over time." (p. 34) Lederach expresses the relational context in which peacebuilding among neighbors sharing the same geographical space and history takes place toward an increase in justice and peace in relationships at a "pace of presence" in the spirit of "alongsidedness" over time. (p. 35).

402 Although I acknowledge the power of technology to advance gospel expressions of faith, spiritual formation, and theological education, I have chosen to focus on local neighbors to offer a humble critique to contrast with online affinity groups that can easily become theologically homogeneous, echo-chambers. The actual physicality of local neighbors grounded in community land makes interactions with diverse people more random and less controlled opportunities for spiritually formative loving engagement (or not). Although avoidable, these everyday interactions with neighbors are still inescapable in exposing our interior resistances to moving with love with real people who can be disagreeable just like us. Visibly embodied spiritual transformation takes place among

Concluding Reflections

When I consider the Jesus Way of the future, I cannot ignore the Barna Group research findings through the current pandemic concerning our Millennial and Gen Z children of faith. Millennial and Gen Z generations do not seem to be interested in status quo church as the Jesus Way of the future. After the Covid-19 pandemic is over, the majority of these younger generation do not prefer returning to in-person gatherings in traditional churches. "They're not walking away from God; they're walking away from church culture."[403] Still, Millennials desire authentic relational cultures with deeper dialogue about morality, values, and how to "read/interpret/study the Bible," through leaders who are "facilitators."[404] Millennials already lead the way in glocal social justice initiatives.[405] Unlike Millennials, Gen Z's "rarely associate negative emotions with faith-sharing," but lean toward relational and embodied faith encounters through mutual, dialogical storytelling and lived-out action.[406] Most Gen Z's consider an engaging witness to be "someone who listens without judgment" and who seems comfortable about their faith, yet they do not consider church to be "a safe space to express doubt" about difficult topics.[407] Young affirms this

---

physical neighbors in actual communities in tangible communal ways in real time and real space as a witness to Jesus Christ as the Way.

403   Barna Group, "Church Pulse Weekly Conversations: Ben Windle on Leading Millennials," citing Ben Windle, June 30, 2021, available online: https://www.barna.com/research/cpw-windle/; accessed March 1, 2022.; Barna Group, "Guest Column: Carey Nieuwhof on Generational Preferences for In-Person Worship Post-Covid," November 11, 2020, available online: https://www.barna.com/preference-for-in-person-worship-services/; accessed March 1, 2022. According to a recent Barna study, "only 41 percent of Gen Z say that when COVID is over, they want to return to primarily in-person worship. 42 percent of Millennials say they prefer primarily in-person worship. Which means, of course, that the majority don't."

404   Barna Group, "Church Pulse Weekly Conversations," citing Ben Windle, June 30, 2021.

405   Mody, "Millennials Leave Shift Away," December 31, 2021. Social justice interests of millennials include immigrant rights and racial justice, among other issues.

406   Barna Group, "Actions, Invitations, Storytelling—How Gen Z Approaches Evangelism," July 27, 2021, available online: https://www.barna.com/research/gen-z-evangelism/; accessed March 1, 2022.

407   Barna Group, "What Makes an Engaging Witness, as Defined by Gen Z," November 10, 2021, available online: https://www.barna.com/research/gen-z-witness/; accessed March 1, 2022.

exodus from church culture as "the growing number of people who were raised in evangelical families [but] now find themselves theologically and religiously 'homeless'."[408] Perhaps this proposed experimental approach for the Jesus Way forward corresponds with the spiritual longings in the hearts of our spiritual children.

As I reflect on this experimental Contemplative Discovery Approach as an embodied Jesus Way for the future, I am struck once again with the stories and parables of Jesus—especially his earthy, agrarian metaphors of sowing and reaping, of gathering and scattering, of seeds and vines. Mustard seeds, tiny and unimpressive, echo back to prophetic words about small beginnings—something not to be despised. I recall Heath's prophetic words of hope as I wonder about and examine the grass and roots in my own neighborhood, reimagining kingdom possibilities. She says, "… it looks like a spiritual dandelion explosion as far as the eye can see. God's new thing is networked, exponential, Spirit-breathed, decentralized, a vast planting of small communities of faith that birth small communities of faith that continue to multiply. It is very much the work of laypeople, and it is emerging as a natural progression out of the church that used to be."[409]

As I reimagine the Jesus Way of the future, I share Heath's vision. For over fifteen years, as a grassroots practitioner, I've been involved in multiple, small but diverse, organic gatherings of Church with marginalized

---

408 Mark S. Young, *The Hope of the Gospel: Theological Education and the Next Evangelicalism* (Grand Rapids, MI: William B. Eerdmans Publishing Company, 2022), p. 23. Published as I was finishing my thesis, Mark S. Young, president of Denver Seminary, released his book in the *Theological Education Between the Times* series. Counterintuitively, Young suggests that evangelicalism's values for pragmatism, its high esteem for scripture, as well as its propensity for revivalism, make it a conducive conduit for revitalizing widespread theological change for the future. pp. 19-23. Interestingly, some evangelical parachurch organizations focusing on the next generation of faith leaders (including FCA and CRU) have begun using various forms of Discovery Bible Study in recent years. See Fellowship of Christian Athletes, *E 3 Play Book* (Kansas City, MO: The Fellowship of Christian Athletes, 2020), pp. 31-35, and Elliott Dodge, "How to Reach the World With a New Style of Bible Study," (March 29, 2017), available online: https://www.cru.org/us/en/train-and-grow/bible-studies/how-to-reach-the-world-with-a-new-kind-of-bible-study.html; accessed March 5, 2022.

409 Heath, *God Unbound*, p. 98.

people.[410] Living on the outskirts of Cleveland, Ohio, we experience the effects of being one of the topmost "hyper-segregated" cities in the United States (See Appendix D).[411] Rated in 2020 as the sixth most segregated city in the United States, with the eighth most segregated metropolitan region, structural racism seems unbearable and impenetrable.[412] The barriers between people and neighborhoods and the complexity of socio-political issues and systemic injustice seem insurmountable. Local institutional churches are just as hyper-segregated, reflective our regional socio-cultural

---

410 These DBS groups have included Millennial/Gen Z young adult groups, Spanish-speaking groups of both documented and undocumented Mexican immigrants, ethnically and racially diverse groups of English speakers, and a Farsi/English speaking group. Venues have included public space and community buildings in impoverished urban neighborhoods, homes in rural settings, Sunday schools and life groups in churches and neighborhood homes, and businesses such as coffee shops and restaurants, as well as online and hybrid groups via Zoom. In addition, faith-based community leaders and pastors have been trained in DBS and/or experimented with contemplative approaches using DBS through youth camps, workshops, Selah School of Contemplative Activism which uses IRPJ online short course for grassroots theological training (https://selahspiritualwellness.com/activism) and through the Cleveland cohort of Sustainable Faith's School of Mercy and Justice (https://sustainablefaith.com/smj-overview/). Other more prominent grassroots theological training programs have arisen nationally as similar alternative theological training grounds for laypeople highlighting contemplative practices and/or DBS, including the Tampa Underground (https://www.tampaunderground.com), the People's Seminary (https://www.peoplesseminary.org), St. Anthony's Institute (https://st-anthony.thinkific.com/collections), and the Neighborhood Seminary (https://www.neighborhoodseminary.org).

411 Vince Grzegorek, "New Data Map Reminds Us Cleveland is Hyper-Segregated," *Scene*, May 10, 2018, available online: https://www.clevescene.com/cleveland/new-data-map-reminds-us-cleveland-is-hyper-segregated/Content?oid=18297703); accessed March 1, 2022. Grzegorek cites a 2016 article referring to Massey's research about hypersegregation where "the minority population is slotted tightly into a specific geographical location," and its far-reaching, isolating effects of racial bifurcation. "Hyper-segregation creates the kind of social and economic isolation that pools poverty and cuts off these parts of a city from the mainstream civic bloodstream, creating the harsh differences between locations separated by a 15-minute drive. Imagine the psychological blow of living close to the Cleveland skyline in the Flats or downtown. Then imagine living on the boarded-up blocks deep on the east side that look like Sarajevo after Milosevic."; Sandel, *Tyranny of Merit*, p. 226. Sandel's words ring true in places like Cleveland, Ohio. He states, "Those who are affluent and those of modest means rarely encounter one another in the course of the day. We live and work and shop and play in different places; our children go to different schools." One look at the map in Appendix D invites and inspires faithful visionaries in my region to hopefully reimagine the alternative beloved community gathering at these sites of segregation for fruitful experimentation to make visible a better, spiritually embodied Way forward for the Church.

412 Menendian, Stephen, Gambhier, Samir, and Hsu, Chih-Wei, "Roots of Structural Racism: The 2020 Census Update," *Othering and Belonging Institute*, University of Berkeley, Berkeley, CA, October 11, 2021, available online: https://belonging.berkeley.edu/roots-structural-racism-2020; accessed March 5, 2022.

milieu. Spiritual inertia is deeply entrenched within our societal injustices, and there is a need for more nimble and flexible expressions of faith in neighborhoods for loving neighbors in order to facilitate compassionate relational healing and to build peace locally.

Radical hospitality in highly segregated communities like my own must begin very small and mustard-seedlike in safe relational spaces like homes where the "new family" can form and be trusted without fear of abuse—be it racial, ethnic, gender, economic, or spiritual. Such "new families of love" foster spiritual recovery and collective trauma healing among neighbors.[413] The Spirit of Jesus comes to the small places where a few gather together, and spiritual conversations are not contrived but transformative. Prayerful seeking through scripture together is natural in the context of loving neighborly connection and welcomed by Jesus who is present in the midst of small gatherings as Host and Guest and Feast.[414] With a christotelic interpretation of scripture, Jesus himself is not marginalized from the Bible. The Spirit recenters and reveals Jesus as the cruciform good news that demonstrates the heart of our Father who is love. The self-giving love of God freely outpours through his beloved family in an embodied love for neighbor that is visible and practical and healing amidst a suffering world to bring faith, hope, and love that one day, everything wrong will be made right. Life-giving reimagining is unleashed in the Spirit and rebirthed in communities with artistic creativity optimal for a revitalizing movement of God.[415]

---

413 The burgeoning fields of research in collective trauma healing and neurotheology document the contribution of contemplative practices for healing. Two noteworthy resources include: Bessel A. Van Der Kolk, *The Body Keeps the Score: Brain, Mind, and Body in the Healing of Trauma* (New York: Penguin Books, 2014), and Resmaa Menakem, *My Grandmother's Hands: Racialized Trauma and the Pathway to Mending Our Hearts and Bodies* (Las Vegas, NV: Central Recovery Press, 2017).

414 Matthew 18:20.

415 The emerging field of theopoetics and increasing interest in aesthetic Christology embraces the creative intersection of beauty, contemplation, and theology. Thoughtful and playful exploration in these theological fields during this time of liminality will enrich and invigorate the future Way. Introductions for consideration can be found in the work of L. Callid Keefe-Perry, *Way to Water: A Theopoetics Primer* (Eugene OR: Cascade Books, 2014) and Chris E.W. Green, *All Things Beautiful: An Aesthetic Christology* (Waco, TX: Baylor University Press, 2021).

These small gatherings do not preclude involvement with the more traditional—and even liturgical—institutional expressions of Church.[416] Relational reciprocity between organic expressions and institutional expressions makes possible the cross-pollination of seeds to mutually revitalize *all* expressions of the embodied Jesus Way as the Body of Christ seeks to move in unity by the Spirit.[417] Organic expressions are networked and decentralized, liked connective tissue among laypeople with various spiritual identities.[418] These groups of laypeople are *un*like monastic orders defined by rules of life because they are open spiritual exchange networks for crossing boundaries and borders to nimbly transcend the religious ideologies that divide us.[419] As prophetic dissent, they embody the Jesus Way, turning so-called "communion" tables that exclude spiritually hungry people from feasting on Jesus in more traditional places.

---

416 Winfield Bevins, *Ever Ancient, Ever New,* pp. 33-42. Bevins' research provides eight reasons why younger generations might be allured to traditional liturgy including: holistic, embodied spirituality; a sense of mystery; a desire for historical rootedness; looking for a countercultural faith; belonging to a universal church; sacramental spirituality; gracious orthodoxy; and finding an anchor in spiritual practice. Certainly, the symbiosis of the organic Contemplative Discovery Approach I suggest meshes with these alluring features of liturgy as individuals and groups in neighborhoods long for connection with larger corporate worshiping communities.; See also Wilda C. Gafney, *A Women's Lectionary for the Whole Church – Year W* (New York: Church Publishing Incorporated, 2021), p. xii. Gafney states: "Based on the numbers in the Pew Research Center's May 12, 2015, report, 'America's Changing Religious Landscape,' as many as 60 percent of American Christians attend services in churches that use lectionaries." This would include roughly 1.4 billion persons including: Roman Catholics, Orthodox Christians, Anglicans, Episcopalians, Methodists, Presbyterians, Lutherans, and other Reformed traditions as well as some Baptist and congregational churches. Liturgy as a "work of the people" in this present socio-cultural milieu can recreate and unloose new liturgical forms such as Gafney's *Women's Lectionary* and new books of common prayer such as the one authored by Shane Claiborne and Jonathan Wilson-Hartgrove, *Common Prayer Pocket Edition: A Liturgy for Ordinary Radicals* (Grand Rapids, MI: Zondervan, 2012).

417 Ephesians 4:1-6.

418 Heath, *God Unbound,* p. 59. Though living on the edge of the Church and in the margins of communities, Heath imagines these new organic expressions intentionally and firmly connecting with the local institutional expressions to revitalize the Church while remaining accountable to the broad historical orthodoxy that Christianity upholds.

419 Personally as a spiritual director, I am intrigued by the thought of a Neo-Desert Ammas and Abbas placed amidst the religious homelessness and wilderness of neighborhoods-in-isolation to act as persons of peace, navigating the liminal space between organic grassroots expressions of faith and the institutional church. These *anam cara* practitioners are distinct from the neo-monastic movement. Instead they are "spirituality discerners" who ask questions, make observations, and provide hospitality for spiritual wanderers and nomads seeking sheltered refuge and loving spiritual companionship. These Ammas and Abbas would function as gatherers of scattered ones.

Weil suggests that the institutional expressions of the Jesus Way serve as the collective "guardian of dogma" that historically identifies the Church.[420] Church history demonstrates the symbiotic pattern between institutional order and prophetic dissent as a means for propelling the Church forward in the socio-cultural moment. During this current "between the times" liminal space for theological reflection,

> Perhaps, like Weil, not a few of us belong outside religious camps, thereby merging with all of them, to bear prophetic witness to a more expansive, generative, self-giving love than can be contained, preserved, or institutionalized. In the humus of cultural diversity, enriched through Christ-in-us, a smaller yet burgeoning alternative community pulsates with life. Birthed deeply through attentiveness to our present-day realities of suffering brought on through necessity by global pandemic isolation, this beloved family is limber, forming with relational freedom and intimacy everywhere. Deeply rooted underground, yet rapidly growing like grass, a mosaic of neighbors connected through co-suffering divine love meet together...[421]

We must fearlessly welcome creative approaches and experiments for new ways for belonging, being and acting as the Jesus Way of love—anchored in our history, with wings thrust forward into the future. The Body of Christ, in all of our beautiful and broken, already-not-yet expressions of the kingdom of God must unify out of our *love* for God and *love* for neighbor for the common good, notwithstanding our theological

---

420 Simone Weil, *Awaiting God: A New Translation of Attente de Dieu and Lettre a un Religieux*, trans. Bradley Jersak (Abbotsford, BC: Fresh Wind Press, 2012), p. 124. Weil contrasts the institutional church as the collective "guardian of dogma" with the true intimacy that occurs when "two or three gather in Jesus' name" in the loving harmony of Pythagorean friendship. (pp. 96-99; 148-151).

421 Marisa Lapish, "Intellectual Honesty and Scrupulosity: A Reflection on Simone Weil," *Macrina Magazine*, no. 8 (August 21, 2021), available online: https://macrinamagazine.com/issue-8-general/guest/2021/08/21/intellectual-honesty-and-scrupulosity-a-reflection-on-simone-weil/; accessed March 1, 2022.

differences and disagreements.[422] As we do so we will discover and engage a contemplative spirituality that is more Christ-like and Spirit-led—an embodied hermeneutic of love—with potential for building local peace with our diverse neighbors as the Jesus Way of the future.[423]

---

422 Michael J. Sandel, *The Tyranny of Merit*, p. 227. Sandel insists that the common good requires that "citizens from all walks of life encounter one another in common spaces and public places. For this is how to learn to negotiate and abide our differences. And this is how we come to care for the common good." Sandel states that this should also inspire humility: "'There, but for the grace of God, or the accident of birth, or the mystery of fate, go I.' Such humility points to a transcendent future beyond, while anchoring the beloved community of love to the present realities with a more loving, self-giving "generous public life."

423 See Postscript in Appendix E.

BIBLIOGRAPHY

Aleshire, Daniel O. *Beyond Profession: The Next Future of Theological Education.* Grand Rapids, MI: William B. Eerdmans Publishing Company, 2021.

Armas, Kat. *Abuelita Faith: What Women on the Margins Teach Us About Wisdom, Persistence, and Faith.* Grand Rapids, MI: Brazos Press, 2021.

Arnold, Eberhard. *Salt and Light: Living the Sermon on the Mount.* Walden, NY: Plough Publishing House, 1998.

Augustine. *The Confessions.* Translated by Maria Boulding. New York: Vintage Books, 1998.

———*On Christian Doctrine.* 1.36.40. www.ntslibrary.com/PDF%20 Books/Augustine%20doctrine.pdf.Accessed on February 16, 2022.

Barna Group. "Actions, Invitations, Storytelling—How Gen Z Approaches Evangelism." July 27, 2021. https://www.barna.com/research/ gen-z-evangelism/.Accessed March 1, 2022.

———"Church Pulse Weekly Conversations: Ben Windle On Leading Millennials." June 30, 2021. https://www.barna.com/research/ cpw-windle/.Accessed March 1, 2022.

———"Guest Column: Carey Nieuwhof on Generational Preferences for In-Person Worship Post-Covid." November 11, 2020. https:// www.barna.com/preference-for-in-person-worship-services/. Accessed March 1, 2022.

———"What Makes an Engaging Witness as Defined by Gen Z." November 10, 2021. https://www.barna.com/research/gen-z-witness/. Accessed March 1, 2022.

Barton, Ruth Haley. *Sacred Rhythms: Arranging our Lives for Spiritual Transformation.* Downers Grove, IL: IVP Books, 2006.

Bass, Alden. "Bringing It To Completion: American New Monastics and the Benedictine Option," *American Benedictine Review* 66, (2015): 352-363. (PDF) "'Bringing it to Completion': American New Monasticism and the Benedictine Tradition," American Benedictine Review 66 (2015): 352-363. | Alden Bass - Academia.edu. Accessed November 10, 2021.

Bass, Diana Butler. *Christianity After Religion: The End of Church and the Birth of a New Spiritual Awakening.* New York: HarperOne, 2012.

Boss, Pauline. *Ambiguous Loss: Learning to Live With Unresolved Grief.* Cambridge, MA: Harvard University Press, 1999.

Bevins, Winfield. *Ever Ancient, Ever New: The Allure of Liturgy for a New Generation.* Grand Rapids, MI: Zondervan, 2019.

Blumhardt, Christoph Friedrich. *Everyone Belongs to God: Discovering the Hidden Christ.* Walden, NY: Plough Publishing House, 2015.

Bonhoeffer, Dietrich. *Life Together: The Classic Exploration of Christian Community.* New York: Harper & Row Publishers, 1954.

Brueggemann, Walter. *Biblical Perspectives on Evangelism: Living in a Three-Storied Universe.* Nashville: Abingdon Press, 1993.

———*The Prophetic Imagination.* Minneapolis: Fortress Press, 2012.

Byassee, Jason. *Surprised by Jesus Again.* Grand Rapids, MI: William B. Eerdmans Publishing Company, 2019.

Calhoun, Adele Ahlberg. *Spiritual Disciplines Handbook: Practices That Transform Us.* Downers Grove, IL: IVP Books, 2015.

Chrysostom, John. *Catena on the Acts of the Apostles* 19.9 (CGPNT 3:315). In *Ancient Christian Commentary on Scripture, New Testament V, Acts,* ed. Francis Martin and gen. ed. Thomas C. Oden, 236. Downers Grove, IL: InterVarsity Press, 2006.

————*Homily 27 on First Corinthians.* CHURCH FATHERS: Homily 27 on First Corinthians (Chrysostom) (newadvent.org) Accessed May 19, 2021.

Claiborne, Shane and Wilson-Hartgrove, Jonathan. *Common Prayer Pocket Edition: A Liturgy for Ordinary Radicals.* Grand Rapids, MI: Zondervan, 2012.

Cole, Neil. "Organic Church." In *Perspectives on the World Christian Movement: A Reader.* 4th ed., edited by Ralph D. Winter and Steven C. Hawthorne, 643- 645. Pasadena, CA: William Carey Library, 2009.

Conde-Frazier, Elizabeth. *Atando Cabos: Latinx Contributions to Theological Education.* Grand Rapids, MI: William B. Eerdmans Publishing Company, 2021.

Contagious Disciple Making: Coaching, Community, Communication. https://contagiousdisciplemaking.com. Accessed January 28, 2022.

Day, Keri. *Notes of a Native Daughter: Testifying in Theological Education.* Grand Rapids, MI: William B. Eerdmans Publishing Company, 2021.

Delay, Lisa Colon. *The Wild Land Within: Cultivating Wholeness Through Spiritual Practice.* Minneapolis, MN: Broadleaf Books, 2021.

Discovery Bible Study Guide. "Discovery Bible Study – A Safe Place to See for Yourself What The Bible Says." https://www.dbsguide.org. Accessed January 28, 2022.

Dodge, Elliott. "How to Reach the World With a New Style of Bible Study." March 29, 2017. https://www.cru.org/us/en/train-and-grow/bible-studies/how-to-reach-the-world-with-a-new-style-of-bible-study.html. Accessed March 5, 2022.

Enns, Peter. "Apostolic Hermeneutics and an Evangelical Doctrine of Scripture: Moving Beyond a Modernistic Impasse." *WTJ* 65 (2003): 277.

———*The Bible Tells Me So: Why Defending Scripture Has Made Us Unable to Read It.* New York: HarperOne, 2014.

Fellowship of Christian Athletes. *E 3 Play Book.* Kansas City, MO: Fellowship of Christian Athletes, 2022.

Flood, Derek. *Disarming Scripture: Cherry-picking Liberals, Violence-loving Conservatives And Why We All Need to Learn to Read the Bible Like Jesus Did.* San Francisco: Metanoia Books, 2014.

Flunder, Yvette A. *Where the Edge Gathers: Building a Community of Radical Inclusion.* Cleveland, OH: The Pilgrim Press, 2005.

Gafney, Wilda C. *A Women's Lectionary for the Whole Church – Year W.* New York: Church Publishing Incorporated, 2021.

Gannon, Thomas M. and Traub, George W. *The Desert and the City.* Chicago: Loyola University Press, 1969.

Garrison, David. "Church Planting Movements." In *Perspectives on the World Christian Movement: A Reader.* 4th ed., edited by Ralph D. Winter and Steven C. Hawthorne, 646-648. Pasadena, CA: William Carey Library, 2009.

Gire, Ken. *Seeing What Is Sacred.* Nashville, TN: W Publishing Group, 2006.

Gonzalez, Justo L. *The Story of Christianity: The Early Church to the Present Day.* Vol. 1. Peabody, MA: Prince Press, 2001.

Grant, Jacquelyn. *White Women's Christ and Black Women's Jesus: Feminist Christology and Womanist Response.* Atlanta, GA: Scholars Press, 1989.

Green, Chris E.W. *All Things Beautiful: An Aesthetic Christology.* Waco, TX: Baylor University Press, 2021.

_____*Sanctifying Interpretation: Vocation, Holiness, and Scripture.* 2nd ed. Cleveland, TN: CPT Press, 2020.

Grzegorek, Vince. "New Data Map Reminds Us Cleveland is Hyper-Segregated." *Cleveland Scene.* May 10, 2018. https://www.clevescene.com/cleveland/new-data-map-reminds-us-cleveland-is-hyper-segregated/Content?oid=18297703. Accessed March 1, 2022.

Hall, Christopher A. *Reading Scripture with the Church Fathers.* Downers Grove, IL: InterVarsity Press, 1998.

Heath, Elaine A. *God Unbound: Wisdom From Galatians for the Anxious Church.* Nashville, TN: Upper Room Books, 2016.

_____*The Healing Practice of Celebration.* Nashville, TN: Abingdon Press, 2020.

_____*The Mystic Way of Evangelism: A Contemplative Vision for Christian Outreach.* Grand Rapids, MI: Baker Academic, 2017.

Hendricks Jr., Obery M. *Christians Against Christianity: How Right-Wing Evangelicals Are Destroying Our Nation and Our Faith.* Boston: Beacon Press, 2021.

Holmes, Barbara A. *Crisis Contemplation: Healing the Wounded Village.* Albuquerque, NM: CAC Publishing, 2021.

Iati, Marisa. "The Pandemic Has Caused Nearly Two Years of Collective Trauma. Many People Are Near A Breaking Point." *Washington Post,* December 24, 2021. https://www.washingtonpost.com/health/2021/12/24/collective-trauma-public-outbursts/. Accessed January 20, 2022.

Jenkins, Philip. *The Next Christendom: The Coming of Global Christianity.* Revised and Expanded Edition. New York: Oxford University Press, 2007.

Jennings, Willie James. *Acts: A Theological Commentary on the Bible.* Louisville, KY: Westminster John Knox Press, 2017.

_____*After Whiteness: An Education in Belonging.* Grand Rapids, MI: William B. Eerdmans Publishing Company, 2020

Jersak, Bradley. *A More Christlike Way: A More Beautiful Faith.* Pasadena, CA: Plain Truth Ministries, 2019.

_____*A More Christlike Word: Reading Scripture the Emmaus Way.* New Kensington, PA: Whitaker House, 2021.

Jordan, Mark D. *Transforming Fire: Imagining Christian Teaching.* Grand Rapids, MI: William B. Eerdmans Publishing Company, 2021.

Justin Martyr. *First Apology* 67. Translated by Marcus Dods and George Reith. Moscow, ID: Roman Roads Media, 2015. Justin MartyV1-0.pdf (romanroadsstatic.com) Accessed May 19, 2021.

Keefe-Perry, Callid L. *Way to Water: A Theopoetics Primer.* Eugene, OR: Cascade Books, 2014.

Lapish, Marisa. "Intellectual Honesty and Scrupulosity: A Reflection on Simone Weil." *Macrina Magazine.* No. 8 (August 21, 2021) https://macrinamagazine.com/issue-8-general/guest/2021/08/21/intellectual-honesty-and-scrupulosity-a-reflection-on-simone-weil/. Accessed March 1, 2022.

_____"The Lord's Supper Table as Icon of Remembrance." *Kenarchy Journal* 3.7 (2022): 133-143. https://www.kenarchy.org/wp-content/uploads/2022/01/Kenarchy_Volume3.7.pdf. Accessed February 16, 2022.

Lederach, John Paul. "Cultivating Peace: A Practitioner's View of Deadly Conflict and Negotiation." In *Contemporary Peacemaking: Conflict, Violence, and Peace Processes.* Edited by John Darby and Roger MacGinty. New York: Palgram MacMillan, 2003: 30-37.

Limouris, Gennadios. "The Eucharist as the Sacrament of Sharing: An Orthodox Point of View." *The Ecumenical Review* (1986): 401-415.

Lohfink, Gerhard. *Jesus and Community: The Social Dimension of Faith.* Translated by John P. Galvin. Philadelphia: Fortress Press, 1984.

Luu, Phuc. *Jesus of the East: Reclaiming the Gospel for the Wounded.* Harrisonburg, VA: Herald Press, 2020.

Maden, Bruce. "God is in the Neighbourhood." *Spiritual Growth Ministries,* (2006): 1-21. https://sgm.org.nz/uploads/2/0/1/6/20165561/god_is_in_the_neighborhood_-_bruce_maden.pdf. Accessed February 23, 2022.

McCaulley, Esau. *Reading While Black: African American Biblical Interpretation as an Exercise of Hope.* Downers Grove, IL: IVP Academic, 2020.

Menakem, Resmaa. *My Grandmother's Hands: Racialized Trauma and the Pathway to Mending Our Hearts and Bodies.* Las Vegas, NV: Central Recovery Press, 2017.

Menendian, Stephen, and Gambhier, Samir, and Hsu, Chih-Wei. "Roots of Structural Racism: The 2020 Census Update." October 11, 2021. *Othering and Belonging Institute,* University of Berkeley, Berkeley, CA. https://belonging.berkeley.edu/roots-structural-racism-2020. Accessed March 5, 2022.

Miles, Sara. *Take This Bread: The Spiritual Memoir of a Twenty-First-Century Christian.* New York: Ballantine Books, 2007.

Mody, Seema. "Millennials Lead Shift Away From Organized Religion As Pandemic Tests Americans' Faith." www.cnbc.com . December 31, 2021. https://www.cnbc.com/2021/12/29/millennials-lead-shift-away-from-organized-religion-as-pandemic-tests-faith.html. Accessed January 20, 2022.

Moore, Charles E. Introduction to *Everyone Belongs to God: Discovering the Hidden Christ,* by Christoph Friedrich Blumhardt. Walden, NY: Plough Publishing House, 2015.

Moore, Osheta. *Dear White Peacemakers: Dismantling Racism with Grit and Grace.* Harrisonburg, VA: Herald Press, 2021.

Moyaert, Marianne. *Fragile Identities: Towards a Theology of Interreligious Hospitality.* Amsterdam: Rodopi, 2011.

Onion, Amanda, Sullivan, Missy, and Mullen, Matt, eds. "Pandemics That Changed History," www.history.com. December 21, 2021. https://www.history.com/topics/middle-ages/pandemics-timeline. Accessed January 20, 2022.

Penner, Glenn M. *In the Shadow of the Cross: A Biblical Theology of Persecution and Discipleship.* Bartlesville, OK: Living Sacrifice Books, 2004.

Pohl, Christine D. *Making Room: Recovering Hospitality as a Christian Tradition.* Grand Rapids, MI: William B. Eerdmans Publishing Company, 1999.

Ponzetti, James Jr. "Renewal in Catholic Community Life and New Monasticism: The Way Of a Contemporary Religious Communal Movement." *The Journal for the Sociological Integration of Religion and Society* 4, no. 2 (Fall 2014): 35-50. https://www.academia.edu/19731771/Renewal_in_Catholic_community_life_and_New_Monasticism_The_way_of_a_contemporary_religious_communal_movement?a. Accessed November 10, 2021.

Puhalo, Lazar. *The Mirror of Scripture: The Old Testament Is About You.* Abbotsford, BC: St. Macrina Press, 2018.

Samson, William. "The Finkenwalde Project." *Monasticism Old and New.* Waco, TX: The Center for Christian Ethics at Baylor University, (2010): 19-25. https://www.baylor.edu/content/services/document.php/116020.pdf. Accessed November 10, 2021.

Sandel, Michael J. *The Tyranny of Merit: Can We Find the Common Good?* New York: Picador, 2020.

Schmemann, Alexander. *The Eucharist: Sacrament of the Kingdom.* Crestwood, NY: St. Vladimir's Seminary Press, 2003.

Sittser, Gerald L. *Water From a Deep Well: Christian Spirituality From Early Martyrs to Modern Missionaries.* Downers Grove, IL: IVP Books, 2007.

Smith, Ted A. *Theological Education Between the Times* book series. Grand Rapids, MI: William B. Eerdmans, 2020 – 2022.

Spielmann, Richard M. *History of Christian Worship.* New York: The Seabury Press, 1966.

Stark, Rodney. *The Rise of Christianity: How the Obscure, Marginal Jesus Movement Became The Dominant Religious Force in the Western World in a Few Centuries.* San Francisco: HarperSanFrancisco, 1997.

Sun, Chloe. *Attempt Great Things for God: Theological Education in Diaspora.* Grand Rapids, MI: William B. Eerdmans Publishing Company, 2020.

Thurman, Howard. *Jesus and the Disinherited.* Boston: Beacon Press, 1976.

Trousdale, Jerry. *Miraculous Movements.* Nashville, TN: Thomas Nelson, 2012.

Van Der Kolk, Bessel. *The Body Keeps Score: Brain, Mind, and Body in the Healing of Trauma.* New York: Penguin Books, 2014.

Voskamp, Ann. *One Thousand Gifts.* Grand Rapids, MI: Zondervan, 2010.

Watson, David L. and Watson, Paul D. "A Movement of God Among the Bhojpuri of North India." In *Perspectives on the World Christian Movement: A Reader* 4th ed., edited by Ralph D. Winter and Steven C. Hawthorne, 697-700. Pasadena, CA: William Carey Library, 2009.

———*Contagious Disciplemaking: Leading Others on a Journey of Discovery.* Nashville, TN: Thomas Nelson, 2014.

Weil, Simone. *Awaiting God: A New Translation of Attente de Dieu and Lettre a un Religieux*. Trans. Bradley Jersak. Abbotsford, BC: Fresh Wind Press, 2012.

Williams, Rowan. "The Bible Today: Reading and Hearing." In *Transcript from the Larkin-Stuart Lecture at a special joint Convocation of Trinity and Wycliffe colleges in Toronto, Canada,* April 16, 2007. https://rowanwilliams.archbishopofcanterbury.org/articles.php/2112/the-bible-today-reading-hearing-the-larkin-stuart-lecture.html. Accessed October 28, 2021.

Winter, Ralph D. and Hawthorne, Steven C., eds. *Perspectives on the World Christian Movement: A Reader.* 4th ed. Pasadena, CA: William Carey Library, 2009.

Wirzba, Norman. *Food and Faith: A Theology of Eating.* 2nd ed. Cambridge, UK: Cambridge University Press, 2020.

Wright, N.T. *Acts for Everyone: Part 1.* Louisville, KY: Westminster John Knox Press, 2008.

Yong, Amos. *Hospitality and the Other: Pentecost, Christian Practices, and the Neighbor.* Maryknoll, NY: Orbis Books, 2008.

———*Renewing the Church by the Spirit: Theological Education After Pentecost.* William B. Eerdmans Publishing Company, 2020.

Young, Mark S. *The Hope of the Gospel: Theological Education in the Next Evangelicalism.* Grand Rapids, MI: William B. Eerdmans Publishing Company, 2022.

Zodhiates, Spiros and Baker, Warren, eds. *Hebrew-Greek Key Word Study Bible: New International Version.* Chattanooga, TN: AMG Publishers, 199

DISCOVERY BIBLE STUDY

Study Guide[424]

DISCOVERY BIBLE STUDY

Study Guide

Talk   25%
What are you thankful for?
What is causing you stress?
Who needs our help? How can we help them?

Look back (session 2+)
Retell story from the previous meeting.
What did you do differently because of this story?
Who did you tell and what was the reaction?

Read & Retell   50%
One person reads the new Bible passage out loud, and the rest follow along.
Someone else retells the story and others fill in what is missing.

Read & Look
Read the passage again.
Discuss what this passage says about **God, Jesus or his plan**.

Read & Look Again
Read the passage once more.
Discuss what this passage says about **humans**.

Inside me   25%
According to this study, what am I doing well?
What do I need to change?

Who else?
Who needs to hear this story, and how can I tell them?
Who can I invite to study the Bible?

---

424 Discovery Bible Study Guide (pdf) on "Discovery Bible Study: A Safe Place to See for Yourself What the Bible Says,"; available online: https//www.dbsguide.org; accessed January 28, 2022.

Group guidelines

Read these five guidelines to the group as you begin the first three or four sessions.

1. Everyone shares in sentences, not paragraphs.

2. Focus only on what this passage is saying, not on other passages.

3. Focus only on what this group is seeing.

4. Give people time to respond. Silence is OK.

5. The facilitator should facilitate discussion, not teach.

Facilitator guidelines

1. Keep the session on schedule and complete all sections, though not necessarily all questions.

2. Prepare before by studying passage, looking for main idea, and think of some examples, stories or applications from your own life.

3. Respond to questions by asking group, "What in the passage helps us answer that question?"

4. Respond to distracting comments by asking, "Where is that found in this passage?"

5. Respond to "strange" answers by asking, "Help us understand what you are thinking."

CONTEMPLATIVE DISCOVERY APPROACH[425]

TALK:

*Contemplative Questions (*Examen*):

1. Think back over your past week. What was life-giving to you this week and makes you thankful? What drained you of life this week and makes you feel stressful?

*Storytelling: (A brief *Silencio* in between stories and testimonies is given to honor each person)

1. Share something that you are thankful for and something that you feel stressed about.
2. Alternatively, ask a storytelling question based on a theme that comes up in the scripture narrative: Tell a story about a time in your life when you experienced deep love? Freedom? Fear? Awe? Suffering? Healing? Confusion?

*Testimonies: (Session 2+)

1. Who did you tell the previous scripture story to and what was the reaction?
2. What changed in your life (in perspective or in action) because of the story?

---

425 This contemplative approach is an example that modifies the original DBS model found as a downloadable pdf for public use available online: https://www.dbsguide.org; accessed January 28, 2022.

READ and RETELL: *(Lectio Divina)*

*Contemplative Prompt for **Lectio**:* (Read scripture in the languages of the people present.)

1.   Imagine yourself in this scene as it is read aloud. What do your senses see, hear, smell, taste, and feel? Notice if you identify with a particular character in the scene or are just an observing bystander. What emotions, body sensations and thoughts do you experience as the story unfolds?

Retell the Story as if you were there. Others are invited to fill in missing details from the story.

1.   Tell the story as the narrator or tell it in first person.
2.   Dramatize the story or draw the scene and tell the story from the picture.

READ and LOOK:

*Contemplative Prompt for **Meditatio for the Literal Sense:***

1.   As the passage is read aloud a second time, take notice of what this passage says about the character and nature of God (or Jesus). Also take notice of what this passage says about the character and nature of people.

Discussion Questions for the *Literal Sense* of Scripture:

1.   "What does this text intend to refer to, and *how* does it intend to refer to it?[426]

---

426   Jersak, *A More Christlike Way,* p. 119. Jersak quotes N.T Wright, "A Conversation with N.T. Wright: What Do You Mean by 'Literal'?" interview by Dr. Peter Enns, The BioLogos Foundation, September 8, 2010, video, 4:29, https://youtu.be/fxQpFosrTUk.

2. "What is the text as a full unit trying not to say or to deny?"[427] Where is this text's movement?[428]
3. What did this passage say about the character and nature of God (Jesus)?
4. What did this passage say about the character and nature of people?

READ and LOOK AGAIN:

*Contemplative Prompt for *Oratio for the Spiritual Sense:*

1. In this third reading, prayerfully ask the Spirit to reveal or point to Christ and his gospel through the scripture. Notice who speaks with the voice of self-giving love and life in this story. With curiosity in the presence of God, imagine how this passage nourishes your spiritual growth as a follower of Jesus Christ to make you more like him.

*Discussion Questions for the *Spiritual Sense* of Scripture: (christotelic, allegorical, moral)

1. How does this story reveal or point to Christ and his gospel?[429] (christotelic, allegorical)
2. Where do you hear the voice of self-giving love and life in this story?[430] (polyphonic christocentric discernment)
3. How will this story nourish my growth as a follower of Jesus Christ?[431] What is the Spirit inviting me toward becoming or doing? What might my next step be? (moral sense)

---

427 Williams, "The Bible Today: Reading and Hearing," pp. 1-5.
428 Ibid.
429 Jersak, *A More Christlike Word,* p. 135. This question is based on Jersak's example of the spiritual/allegorical sense of scripture.
430 Ibid., pp. 193-213. This question is based on Jersak's distinction between voices of self-giving love vs. sacrificial religion.
431 Ibid., p. 132. This question is based on Jersak's example of the moral sense of scripture.

INSIDE ME:

*<u>Contemplative Prompt</u> for ***Contemplatio:***

1. As this passage is read a final time, rest in the divine Presence, re-membering that God will one day restore all things, and he is lovingly beginning that transformation within you and through you to love others in your world. Rest in his healing, restorative presence making all things new.

*<u>Discussion Questions</u> for the *Spiritual Sense* of Scripture: (anagogical)

1. How do you imagine that the small things we shared together today will continue to bring love, faith, and hope that one day all things will be made right? (anagogical sense)
2. How does the Spirit seem to be moving us together to be restorative in our community?

WHO ELSE:

*<u>Action Questions</u> for ***Incarnatio:*** (embodied action *with* the community *in* the community)

1. Who else might be longing to heal together with us through scripture and community?
2. What neighborhoods are calling us to stand in solidarity with them as Jesus would?
3. What healing, reconciliation, or recovery can we be contributors to for restoration in our local community?

(See Appendix C for examples of additional discussion questions or create ones of your own.)

Appendix C

CONTEMPLATIVE DISCOVERY APPROACH

Additional Discussion Questions[432]

Examples of additional questions for discussion to evoke the *literal* sense of scripture:

1. What is the genre of this passage (or book of the Bible)? What historical or cultural context would help us to understand this text more clearly? (Suggest outside resources for discovery and exploration.)
2. What truth does the author of the passage convey?
3. What does it seem God desires to restore in this passage?
4. What is God's redemptive path in this passage?
5. How is God described and what is implied by his actions and about his character?
6. Where do you see God (Jesus) *with* the suffering ones and *against* injustice in this passage?
7. Which character in the story might be perceived as a person of privilege and which character suffers most by the actions in this passage?
8. What "tables are turned" by God/Christ's action in this passage to liberate the oppressed person?

---

432 Contributors of these questions include Jen Gallion, Ruth Ringenbach, Isabel Vera Zambrano, and Courtnee White. This group of women participated locally in IRPJ online courses, a book discussion about Jersak's *A More Christlike Word*, various DBS groups, and contemplative practices including lectio divina through the pandemic together.

Examples of additional questions to evoke the *spiritual* sense of scripture:

Christotelic/Allegorical

1. How does Jesus fulfill the truth of this passage?
2. Where do you see the love of Jesus portrayed in this passage?
3. How does this passage reflect the self-giving life, death, resurrection, or reign of Jesus?

(Discernment)

1. In contrast to the voice of self-giving love and life, where in this passage do you hear the voice of the accuser who comes to steal, kill, and destroy?
2. What voice in the text stands out to you as a voice that doesn't quite fit with the person who is speaking?

Moral

1. How will this story transform me so that the truth of my being (the image of Christ) becomes the way of my being (the likeness of Christ)?[433] How am I changing?
2. Is there any action/attitude to be desired and or emulated or vice versa?
3. How can I partner with the Spirit to be part of a redemptive solution in my community?
4. Who might God be inviting me to see, hear, and love?

Anagogical

1. How does this passage give me hope that restoration is taking place?
2. How does this passage give me faith that God is at work to right all wrongs even today?
3. How do I imagine the future kingdom of God reflecting this theme in its fullness?

---

433 Jersak, *A More Christlike God,* p. 132. This question is based on Jersak's example of the moral sense.

APPENDIX D

HYPER-SEGREGATED CLEVELAND MAP[434]

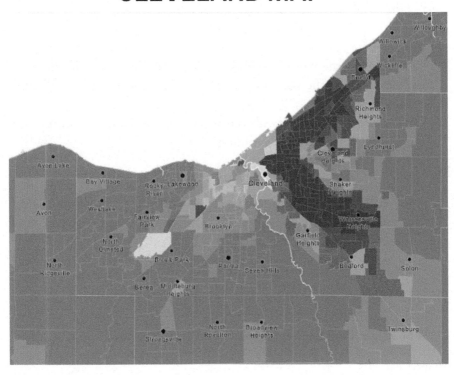

Red: Black population density
Blue: White population density
Green: Asian population density
Orange: Hispanic/Latino population density

---

434 Vince Grzegorek, "New Data Map," May 10, 2018. Image taken from article available online: https://www.clevescene.com/cleveland/new-data-map-reminds-us-cleveland-is=hyper-segregated/Content?oid=18297703; accessed March 1, 2022.

APPENDIX E

POSTSCRIPT

On February 24, 2022, Russia invaded Ukraine. As I finished writing, various sources were reporting Russian and Ukrainian war fatalities to be approaching 1000 human beings. With such large scale global war and peace problems at hand, what in the *world* do I think my two cents summarized in these pages could possibly contribute to bringing local peace to my community, let alone have any bearing on the large-scale pain and collective trauma everywhere in the world? It felt like a mere drop in the bucket, to say the least....and a mustard-seed to say the most.

And then, I remembered the Jesus Way...

> Before we can love our neighbor, we must see our neighbor and hear our neighbor. Observing the way a gardener observes plants. Watching their buds when they're blooming. Watering their roots when they're wilting. But we cannot weep with those who weep or rejoice with those who rejoice unless we first see something of their tears or hear something of their laughter. If we can learn to see and hear our neighbor, maybe, just maybe, we can learn to see and hear God. And seeing him, and hearing, Him, to love Him. To passionately love God and other people. This is what matters. This is *all* that matters.[435]

The Jesus Way is love, hovering and blowing like wind wherever it will, near and far, scattering good news as neighbors share heirloom mus-

---

435 Ken Gire, *Seeing What is Sacred* (Nashville, TN: W Publishing Group, 2006), p. 77.

tard seeds, from one neighbor's garden to the next to plant in organic soil—a community garden for tasting and seeing that the Lord is good. [436]

I cringed, recalling the first time my elderly neighbor shouted off her porch to me while I was weeding out dandelions in my flower bed. Her derogatory, racist words, intended to be a joke, scorched my heart: "Are you Mexican? Can you come over and weed my flower beds too?" Helen laughed out loud. Through the winter, I forced myself to extend neighborly love to her through random acts of kindness, in the form of soup and bread and Christmas cookies as my husband shoveled her driveway and swept off her porch. But I just couldn't shake or forget her former disparaging remarks. She was appreciative of the food though, and frequently invited me inside for a visit. Every time I excused myself, saying that I was on my way elsewhere or busy doing something else. I just couldn't bear the thought of the direction the conversation might go and had no energy to listen to racist comments about my friends. Frankly, I wasn't really interested in listening to her story.

Just two weeks ago, when she texted to thank me for some soup, Helen apologized that she couldn't make it to the door because her doctor had just put her on oxygen and she couldn't get down the stairs fast enough, as I dropped off another bowl of soup, rang the doorbell, and hurried back to my house. A seed of compassion was planted in my heart when I heard about her declining health, and I told her I had a loaf of bread that I would drop off later that day. I could see Helen through the window, waiting for me in her rocking chair, when I got to the door. I rang the doorbell and she once again invited me to come in. This time I joined her at her kitchen table to eat some bread. Our conversation went like this...

Helen: Are you Mexican?

Me: No, my background is mostly Italian. Why do you ask?

Helen: Your soup is always so spicy, and I always see Mexicans going in and out of your door.

Me: Oh yes, I have friends who are Mexican. Next time I can make the soup less spicy if you would like it better that way.

---

436 Psalm 34:8.

Helen: Do you run a soup kitchen for the elderly or something?

Me: (laughing), Oh no, we just like to eat soup in the winter, and I had a little extra.

Helen: Then you must be Catholic because only Catholics do nice things for people. But listen to me… You have to make sure you don't get involved doing anything special for those neighbors across the street though. They're alcoholics and will take advantage of you. (Pause) And Kate next door tells me that the reason you're always on your back porch reading books and on your computer is because you go to school. Why in the world at your age would you go to school?

Me: (smiling) Sometimes I wonder the same thing, Helen.

Helen: So what are you studying anyway?

Me: Theology and Culture with a focus on Peace Studies.

Helen: Why in the HELL would you ever study that?

Me: Well, Helen…don't you think our world needs a little more peace and love these days?

[*My God*, how I'm growing to love my Ukrainian neighbor, Helen…]

~Selah~

And so God's love story continues to scatter little seeds of good news—life-giving words implanted in organic neighborhood soil to transform strangers into neighbors and enemies into family as we gather around tables, sharing stories, praying under our breath, eating bread...

ACKNOWLEDGMENTS

This book, in many respects, is the culmination of my own spiritual journey as a disciple of the Jesus Way. My words are a reflection of the *eucharisteo*—thanksgiving—I carry in my heart today on this leg of my pilgrimage. In this spirit, I offer my deep gratitude to...

~Chris E. W. Green, my thesis supervisor, who inspired me through his theological writing to see that our spiritual heritage has value in spiritual formation, urging us forward as peacemakers for the common good in our communities.

~Bradley Jersak, my "second reader," professor, and Dean, who with humility and kindness challenged me to deep reflection, beyond the spectrum of our religious ideologies, to transcend them through love. Thank you for encouraging me to contemplatively write with a christocentric lens.

~Andrew Klager, director of the IRPJ and professor, whose generosity and encouragement models for me the inner transformation of a peacemaker.

~Peter Fitch, Walter Thiessen, Lorna Jones, David Moore, and L.A. Henry, whose instruction at SSU enriched and impassioned me to write.

~Shawna Lucas, Lisa Meier, and Darlene Enns-Dyck, my *anam cara* thesis companions who offered generous space to vent, rant, challenge, and wrestle with ideas—with laughter and tears—and to the rest of my graduate student friends at SSU and the IRPJ.

~Jen Gallion, Ruth Ringenbach, Isabel Vera Zambrano, and Courtnee White, my conversation partners who spurred me on by asking faithful questions, giving valuable insights, and offering deep and intimate friendship.

~Michael Huffman, a dear son in the faith, who prodded me to continue my education and writing exploits and whose reference letter still makes me cry.

~Hazel Partington, Dave Baker, Jen Gallion, Ivonne Pinera, Isabel Vera Zambrano, Kelly and Marie Irish, who faithfully read my thesis chapter by chapter, offering encouragement and helpful comments.

~To the unnamed people in this book who have graciously shared their lives and stories with me.

~The many participants in the Discovery Bible Studies in our community who have inspired me and spiritually formed me.

~Brittany and Charles Wilhelm (and Elia and Zeke), Alyse Nevil and Ryan Nevil (and Gio, Linc, Ollie), Olivia Lapish (and Zamfir), Samuel and Emma Lapish, Phil and Erin Lapish (and Roman), Caleb and Liza Lapish, Elisabeth and Matt Karki, Caroline Lapish, Angelee and Ethan DeLeon, and Gianna Lapish, my beautiful family who supported me in manifold ways throughout my educational journey over the last three years.

~Alyse Nevil and Sam Lapish, my talented grant-writing children whose masterful editing and formatting skills, not to mention our deep theological discussions, have blessed me well beyond the extra mile. You each deserve an honorary graduate degree in theology for your labor of love on my behalf.

~Leon Eiswerth, my dad, who I am forever grateful taught me to be a critical, creative thinker. I love you more.

~Jim Lapish, my husband and love of my life who continually models the beauty and simplicity of the Jesus Way. Thank you for supporting and contributing to my calling through every season of life. The life we have built together is a source of great joy, thanksgiving, and fulfillment for me. I love you forever.

~Thank you, God, "for the love song You keep singing, the gift of Yourself that you keep giving…for the wild wonder of You in this moment."[437]

---

437 Ann Voskamp, *One Thousand Gifts:* (Grand Rapids, MI: Zondervan, 2010), p. 217.

Made in the USA
Monee, IL
04 May 2023

32801718R00085